**John Fletcher** is Emeritus Professor of French and Comparative Literature at the University of East Anglia and Honorary Senior Research Fellow in French at the University of Kent. His publications include *The Novels of Samuel Beckett* (Chatto and Windus, 1964), *Samuel Beckett's Art* (Chatto and Windus, 1967), *Claude Simon and Fiction Now* (Calder and Boyars, 1975) and *Novel and Reader* (Calder and Boyars, 1980).

**Bill Naismith**, the series editor of the Faber Critical Guides, was a Lecturer in Drama at the University of London, Goldsmiths' College, for twenty-five years and now lectures in Drama for the Central University of Iowa in London. His other published work includes Student Guides to *'Top Girls' by Caryl Churchill* (Methuen, 1991), *'The Rover' by Aphra Behn* (Methuen, 1993), *'Across Oka' by Robert Holman* (Methuen, 1994) and *'Our Country's Good' by Timberlake Wertenbaker* (Methuen, 1995).

D0188988

**FABER CRITICAL GUIDES**
Series Editor: Bill Naismith

**BRIAN FRIEL**
(*Philadelphia, Here I Come!*, *Translations*, *Making History*,
*Dancing at Lughnasa*)
by Nesta Jones

**SEAN O'CASEY**
(*The Shadow of a Gunman*, *The Plough and the Stars*,
*Juno and the Paycock*)
by Christopher Murray

**HAROLD PINTER**
(*The Birthday Party*, *The Caretaker*, *The Homecoming*)
by Bill Naismith

**TOM STOPPARD**
(*Rosencrantz and Guildenstern Are Dead*, *Jumpers*, *Travesties*,
*Arcadia*)
by Jim Hunter

# A FABER CRITICAL GUIDE
# Samuel Beckett

*Waiting for Godot*

*Endgame*

*Krapp's Last Tape*

JOHN FLETCHER

*faber and faber*

First published in 2000
by Faber and Faber Limited
3 Queen Square London WCIN 3AU

Photoset by Wilmaset Ltd, Birkenhead, Wirral
Printed in England by Mackays of Chatham plc, Chatham, Kent

All rights reserved
© John Fletcher, 2000

John Fletcher is hereby identified as author
of this work in accordance with Section 77
of the Copyright, Designs and Patents Act 1988

*This book is sold subject to the condition that it shall not,
by way of trade or otherwise, be lent, resold, hired out or
otherwise circulated without the publisher's prior consent in
any form of binding or cover other than that in which it is
published and without a similar condition including this
condition being imposed on the subsequent purchaser*

A CIP record for this book
is available from the British Library
ISBN 978-0-571-19778-1
ISBN 0-571-19778-7

4 6 8 10 9 7 5 3

# Contents

# CONTENTS

# Editor's Preface

The *Faber Critical Guides* provide comprehensive introductions to major dramatists of the twentieth century.

The need to make an imaginative leap when reading dramatic texts is well known. Plays are written with live performance in mind. Often a theatre audience is confronted with a stage picture, a silent character or a vital movement – any of which might be missed in a simple 'reading'. The *Guides* advise you what to look for.

All plays emerge from a context – a background – the significance of which may vary but needs to be appreciated if the original impact of the play is to be understood. A writer may be challenging convention, reacting to the social and political life of the time or engaging with intellectual ideas. The *Guides* provide coverage of the appropriate context in each case.

A number of key texts are examined in each *Guide* in order to provide a sound introduction to the individual dramatists. Studying only one work is rarely enough to make informed judgements about the style and originality of a writer's work. Considering several plays is also the only way to follow a writer's development.

Finally, the *Guides* are meant to be read in conjunction with the play texts. 'The play's the thing' and must always be the primary concern. Not only are all playwrights different but every play has its own distinctive features which the *Guides* are concerned to highlight.

# Abbreviations

COED   *Concise Oxford English Dictionary*
SOED   *Shorter Oxford English Dictionary*
STB    Beckett's own production of *Warten auf Godot* (the German text of *Waiting for Godot*) at the Schiller Theater, Berlin, 1975.
T1, T2 Respectively, the first and second typescript drafts of *Fin de partie*, Beckett's original French version of *Endgame*.

Page references throughout are to the Faber and Faber paperback editions (re-set in 2000) of *Waiting for Godot*, *Endgame*, and *Krapp's Last Tape and Embers*; in the case of other Beckett plays, to the *Complete Dramatic Works*, also published by Faber.

# Introduction

When Samuel Beckett died in December 1989 the event was overshadowed by the momentous happenings in Romania which were occurring at the same time. As part of the collapse of Communism which was sweeping the whole of Eastern Europe, the people of that country overthrew their tyrants, the Ceauşescu family; the hated dictator and his wife were summarily tried and executed. Mr Ceauşescu's obituary appeared in *The Times* on the same day as Beckett's, 27 December, but even then it was clear whose death held real significance: the article about the dramatist took up the top half of the page and the politician's was relegated to the space beneath it.

For, as history teaches us, kings, princes and other potentates come and go, but artists live for ever. Who would now remember the name of the Archbishop of Salzburg for whom Mozart worked in the 1770s if the great composer had not fallen out with him? How much would we know – or care – about the little princesses who lived at the Spanish court in the 1650s if the great painter Velásquez had not been commissioned to do their portraits? So, long after the Ceauşescus have been relegated to a footnote in the history books, Beckett's plays will still be performed around the world and studied in schools and universities everywhere.

This book aims to explain why Beckett's work is so significant and why it will last. When he died at the age of eighty-three he was already seen as one of the truly great literary figures of the twentieth century; his writings for the theatre in particular had made him famous, and the plays that I shall be focusing on here – *Waiting for Godot*, *Endgame* and *Krapp's Last Tape* – had become part of the standard repertoire in theatres all over the world. These and his novels were already considered classics of modern literature and as naturally a part of an educated person's experience as the works of Ibsen or Kafka or James Joyce.

Although he once declared, in an arresting phrase, 'the artist who gambles his being comes from nowhere and has no brothers', Samuel Barclay Beckett (to give him his full name) did have a biography even if he was discreet and self-effacing about personal matters. His deep pessimism – something to which I shall return – led him to consider his birth (at Foxrock, near Dublin, on Good Friday, 13 April 1906) a 'calamity', and yet his childhood was happy enough. His father, William Frank Beckett, was a respected and prosperous Dublin businessman; he and his wife Mary (née Roe) were very fond of their second son, and he of them: their deaths, in 1933 and 1950 respectively, grieved him deeply.

'Willie' Beckett, as the father was affectionately known in Irish business and professional circles, was a cheerful, plump man who much enjoyed taking long walks and sharing jokes with his young son, whose outstanding sporting and academic record, first at school and then at university, made him, an early school-leaver himself, immensely proud. Though like all the family a regular church-goer, Beckett senior was less passionate in his Protestant belief than either his wife or his elder son Frank, who succeeded him at the head of the family firm. As for young Samuel's faith, this did not survive his student days, but Christian mythology was to remain a haunting motif behind his writing from first to last, as we shall see when we come to look more closely at the plays, *Waiting for Godot* in particular.

Willie and Mary Beckett, like all caring parents, wanted the best possible education for their child. He was sent first to Miss Ida Elsner's Academy, a kindergarten near where they lived, and when he was a bit older he commuted by rail to Earlsfort House preparatory school in Dublin. He was to remember this regular journey on the old steam train – mocked by local wits as the 'Dublin Slow and Easy' – many years later in his first and finest play for radio, *All That Fall* (1957). The people who have come to meet their loved ones at the little station at Foxrock which Beckett knew so well are starting to get anxious over the fact that the 12.30 from the city is running strangely late, and so they look to the station-master for an explanation:

MRS ROONEY: Before you slink away, Mr Barrell, please, a statement of some kind, I insist. Even the slowest train on this brief line is not ten minutes and more behind its scheduled time without good cause, one imagines.

MR TYLER: I do think we are owed some kind of explanation, Mr Barrell, if only to set our minds at rest.

MR BARRELL: I know nothing. All I know is there has been a hitch. All traffic is retarded. (pp. 186–7)

When the time came for the young Samuel to start his secondary education his parents decided to send him to the top fee-paying establishment in Ireland, Portora Royal, a Protestant boarding school in County Fermanagh (now part of Northern Ireland). From there he went loaded with academic and sporting honours to university in Dublin, winning a scholarship to read French and Italian at Trinity College, the great Protestant foundation that dates back to the reign of Queen Elizabeth I. Here again he enjoyed an active extra-curricular life, notably in amateur dramatics and in the chess, golf and cricket clubs. He is in fact the only winner of the Nobel Prize for Literature to have played in first-class cricket: *Wisden* records his participation in the Northamptonshire versus Dublin University match in July 1927. In his finals he got the top 'first' of his year and was awarded the distinction of a large gold medal. Some fifty years before him the same prize had been won by another great Irish playwright, Oscar Wilde, who refused to part with the precious object even when poverty-stricken and on his death-bed in Paris.

As one would expect of such a brilliant student, Beckett was marked out by his teachers for an academic career, and as the first step in this direction he was chosen to represent Trinity in the regular scheme for exchanging lectors with the prestigious École Normale Supérieure in Paris. He filled the two-term interval between his finals and the start of his French contract by accepting a temporary teaching post at Campbell College in Belfast. Although he was a Protestant in a majority Protestant community – since by then Ireland had been partitioned – he was not happy in the north, and could not wait to escape to Paris. In fact his family's religion was never an issue when it came to his national identity. To the end of his life he kept his Republic of Ireland passport and never had any doubts that he was an Irishman to the core. He had reservations about such things as the dominance of the Roman Catholic Church in the young Republic, not because it was Catholic

4

(his best friend in Ireland, Thomas McGreevy, was a devout Roman Catholic), but because it was (in his view) an institution that did nothing to discourage the new state from adopting such illiberal and philistine policies as the censorship of books. He was, in other words, a thoroughly patriotic Irishman who found it more congenial to live abroad and return home for family visits.

Beckett took up his post at the École Normale in October 1928. A near-contemporary at the school was the brilliant philosopher and founder of French Existentialism Jean-Paul Sartre, but the two men had little contact. On the other hand Beckett formed a close friendship with a student of English there, Alfred Péron, whose death later in a German concentration camp affected him deeply. But the major event of his two years at the École was the meeting with James Joyce, a fellow-Dubliner who had settled in Paris.

Joyce was old enough to be Beckett's father, and was a Catholic (albeit a lapsed one) of distinctly lower-class origins, so nothing in their backgrounds suggested that they would get on. Moreover, the older man had an exuberant, outgoing temperament whereas the younger was inclined to be taciturn and withdrawn. But Joyce was a genius, and Beckett recognised this at once. He became Joyce's devoted friend and helper (Joyce suffered from very poor eyesight and needed people to read things for him). Although never his secretary, Beckett gave him a lot of assistance in his work and his own writing (which began when he moved to Paris) was for a time influenced by that of the older master. He was particularly impressed by Joyce's single-minded dedication to his art and came to share it, although his own path as a writer soon diverged from his friend's.

On the expiration of his Paris contract in 1930 he returned to Dublin to take up a post as assistant in French to Professor Thomas B. Rudmose-Brown, a cultivated and widely read man who had had a decisive role in forming his literary tastes as an undergraduate. He began publishing literary criticism – his book on the great French novelist Marcel Proust appeared in 1931 – and seemed safely launched on the academic career which he seemed eminently suited for and which his father very much hoped he would make a success of. An echo of this appears in a later novel which he decided to leave unfinished, *From an Abandoned Work*:

> Fortunately my father died when I was a boy, otherwise I might have been a professor, he had set his heart on it. A very fair scholar I was too, no thought, but a great memory. One day I told him about Milton's cosmology, away up in the mountains we were, resting against a huge rock looking out to sea, that impressed him greatly.
>
> (p. 142)

But Beckett soon found that he had no vocation for, and little skill at, university teaching: as he later put it, with characteristic self-deprecation, 'I could not bear the absurdity of teaching others what I did not know myself.' The crisis came during the Christmas vacation of 1931 when he was visiting relatives in Germany, and he telegraphed his resignation. Irresponsible as the act appeared to his family and friends at the time, it was decisive in cutting the umbilical cord with Trinity and the Dublin literary circles in which a lesser man might have been content to accept the pre-eminent place his talents granted him. Not that Beckett ever lost his respect for those Irish painters and poets, such as Jack B. Yeats, Denis Devlin and Thomas McGreevy, whose work he praised in print whenever he was given the opportunity.

The years that followed his abrupt departure from academe were lonely and often unhappy, but they were not wasted. Beckett travelled widely in Europe, in Germany in particular, making himself an expert in the visual arts and in the major European languages and literatures (he later used his connoisseurship to champion neglected painters whom he had befriended, such as Henri Hayden and Bram van Velde). He even lived for a time in London, in Chelsea, where he set his first major novel, *Murphy*, published in 1938. Although he tried subsequently to repudiate most of his early work, Beckett still considered this book the foundation stone of his literary output. Its publication was hardly a triumph, but a few were affected by it – notably the novelist Iris Murdoch, who read it as an undergraduate at Oxford, and who later paid affectionate homage to it in her own first novel, *Under the Net* (1954).

In 1937 he ended his years of wandering and made Paris his permanent home by buying a flat in Montparnasse. Appropriately he is buried not far from the building in which he spent the last decades of his life, in Montparnasse cemetery, alongside many other famous artists and writers, including the greatest of all French poets, Charles Baudelaire. Until the royalties from *Waiting for Godot* made him wealthy, he eked out the annuity which his father had left him by doing literary translations, his skill in this art being highly valued by editors.

The outbreak of the Second World War in 1939 found him vacationing with his family in Dublin; he got back to France just in time, preferring, as he later put it, 'France in war to Ireland at peace'. Because the Irish Republic had

declared itself neutral, his citizenship would have
protected him from molestation in German-occupied
Paris, but influenced by his friend Alfred Péron and his
own distaste for Nazism (which he had seen at first hand
in Germany in the mid-1930s), he chose to join the French
Resistance. His group was infiltrated by a double agent
and betrayed to the Gestapo. Beckett narrowly escaped
arrest and eventually found his way to a small village in
the south of France where he went into hiding, bravely
taking on the job of gathering information about German
troop movements and translating it into English for
onward transmission to London. Had he been caught
with this compromising material, his Irish passport would
not have saved him from the firing squad. Traces of this
dangerous occupation, for which he was decorated after
the war by General de Gaulle, survive in the anxiety the
heroes of his later novels feel about 'writing their report'.
This is Moran speaking in the novel *Molloy*, published in
1951, six years after the war ended:

> A letter from Youdi, in the third person, asking for a
> report. He will get his report ... One day I received a
> visit from Gaber. He wanted the report ... I have
> spoken of a voice telling me things ... It told me to
> write the report ... Then I went back into the house
> and wrote, It is midnight. The rain is beating on the
> windows. It was not midnight. It was not raining.
>
> (pp. 175–6)

The contradiction in the last four sentences betrays the
ambivalence Beckett felt about the espionage he was
called upon to engage in and which he later dismissed as
'boy-scout stuff'. General de Gaulle evidently did not
share his opinion of this wartime work.

The liberation of France in 1944 soon enabled Beckett to resume his Paris existence. There he wrote, almost in an inspired trance, those works in French (later self-translated into English) on which his reputation will permanently rest: the trilogy of novels *Molloy*, *Malone Dies* and *The Unnamable*, and the play *Waiting for Godot*. The burst of creative energy which produced these works petered out in 1950. Nothing he wrote later, with the exception of the plays *Endgame* and *Krapp's Last Tape*, and the late autobiographical prose poem *Company* (1980), was quite to equal the works of the late 1940s in profundity, originality and imaginative power.

In *profundity*, because the trilogy and *Waiting for Godot* probe the big questions of human existence: who are we and why are we here? In *originality*, because Beckett evolved a style which succeeds in balancing comedy and tragedy, the grotesque and the sublime; in fiction it made him the greatest experimenter since Joyce, in the theatre the most influential dramatist since Ibsen. In *imaginative power*, finally, because his finest work attains almost effortlessly to the status of universal myth: the outcast heroes of his novels, like his two clowns waiting beside a road for Godot, the elusive benefactor who never arrives, strike a chord in all of us in this age of doubt and anxiety when none of the age-old certainties of class, family and religion hold sway any longer.

In later years, while continuing to write new drama and prose, and even the occasional poem, Beckett took an increasing interest in the direction of his own plays. His productions of *Waiting for Godot* and *Krapp's Last Tape* at the Schiller Theater in Berlin and of *Happy Days* at the Royal Court in London were the first of many which offered fresh, authoritative readings of works which he simplified and stylised in ways other directors would not have dared. The influence that he has exerted over the modern theatre, both as a writer and director, is immense. Figures as pre-eminent as the playwright Harold Pinter and the director Peter Hall acknowledge the enormous debt they owe him; indeed, theatre people the world over revere him as the greatest modern master of their age-old art.

But, though universally admired and much written about ('Beckett studies' quickly became an academic growth industry, somewhat ironically in the light of Beckett's own misgivings about the efficacy of higher education), he accepted surprisingly few honours and then (the 1969 Nobel Prize in particular) only with reluctance. A modest and unassuming man, he was courteous and generous with people whom he trusted, and intransigent only when it came to upholding standards of production and translation of his writings: he would not hestitate, for instance, to seek legal enforcement of his rights where he felt his work was being travestied in the name of political correctness or in a quest for notoriety (such as all-women casts in plays written for male actors, performances in the nude or in drag, and generally anything not authorised by his carefully detailed and painstakingly explicit stage-directions). He refused steadfastly to don the mantle of the 'great man of letters' that he undoubtedly was, and, at least as far as television and the press were concerned, remained a recluse to the end; unlike many prominent people in the arts world, he never went in for the so-called 'rare interview' to promote his latest book or play.

This was not out of disdain – though he *was* a very shy person – but because in his view literature was too serious a matter to be trifled with; he felt it grotesque to receive personal adulation for giving expression to what he called, in one of his characteristically pithy phrases, 'the issueless predicament of existence'. For, as he wondered in his finest poem,

> who may tell the tale
> of the old man?
> weigh absence in a scale?
> mete want with a span?
> the sum assess
> of the world's woes?
> nothingness
> in words enclose?

The answer is that Samuel Beckett did, with wit, with humility and with a compassion that will ensure his immortality.

# Context and Background

## Modernism and Post-modernism

Unlike most other great playwrights, who have usually left a substantial body of work, Beckett's complete dramatic output can be contained in a single volume, and yet he is recognised – on the basis of this surprisingly slight corpus of plays – to be one of the world's foremost practitioners of the art of writing for the theatre. This is something rather new in the history of the medium. By the time of his death, Beckett had written some three dozen plays, but a high proportion of them can count only as playlets, or what an earlier generation would have called 'curtain-raisers', short pieces that might have come in useful to a theatre manager wishing to fill out a particular programme. Of his full-length plays, the first and most elaborate, *Eleuthéria*, was rejected by its author, and in conformity with the wish he clearly expressed before his death and reiterated in his will, remains unperformed, and is likely to remain so for the foreseeable future; of the others, normally only *Waiting for Godot* is considered able to stand comfortably on its own in an evening programme.

But slight as some of the 'dramaticules' and occasional pieces that Beckett wrote towards the end of his life undoubtedly are, they do reveal a remarkably restless and fertile talent, albeit one that was by then able to operate only in a small and restricted compass. It was not, however, merely his advanced age that prevented Beckett tackling full-length plays any longer: he had, quite consciously and deliberately, written himself out of the normal form. When it was first produced in 1969, *Breath* – which runs for only a few minutes – seemed like a joke or a spoof, and it was indeed that to some extent (Beckett, despite his reputation as a gloomy pessimist, certainly did not lack a sense of humour), but it was also prophetic of things to come. His plays had been getting inexorably shorter all the time. His first attempt at stage writing was *Human Wishes*; intended as a four-act play based on the life of Dr Johnson, it was begun in 1937 and abandoned after only a few pages. *Eleuthéria* is in three acts; *Waiting for Godot* is in two, because, as Beckett rather apologetically put it, 'One act would have been too little and three would have been too much': how astute, how sensible that remark now sounds. *Endgame*, as we shall see, began as a two-act play, but Beckett sensibly dropped the interval when it became clear to him that there was no structural justification for it. Since *Krapp's Last Tape*, with the exception of *Happy Days* (1961), which needs an interval for a purely technical reason (the props-change required to plant Winnie deeper in the ground), all his plays have been one-act, even single-scene, affairs.

There is no intrinsic reason why plays should take two or three hours to perform, of course; the fact that most do is attributable to sociological factors. Until the advent of motion pictures playing to mass audiences in huge cinemas, and later on the installation of a television set in every living room, the theatre, the opera and the music-hall were the standard forms of public entertainment. Since these art forms, unlike cinema and television, came relatively expensive to the individual consumer – and now usually require state subsidy or business sponsorship if they manage to survive at all – the audience expected value for money in the shape of a full evening's entertainment as a return for the outlay on the ticket price. Elaborate evening dress and expensive suppers after the performance all added to the sense of occasion, but also to the cost. Plays, operas and variety shows were therefore created to satisfy the demand for pleasantly distracting ways of filling the time between dinner and supper. Hence the rise of what became known as the 'well-made play' or 'drawing-room comedy': works written by the likes of George Bernard Shaw (1856–1950), J. B. Priestley (1894–1984), Somerset Maugham (1874–1965) and Noël Coward (1899–1973) which engaged the interest of audiences and entertained them without perplexing them unduly or upsetting them too much. The genre survived just so long as did the leisured classes who had the time to enjoy it and the money to pay for it; when their importance and their influence on the leisure market declined, after a short time-lag it fell into desuetude, so that by the time Beckett came on the scene in the 1950s the process was well under way.

But what makes Beckett a great dramatist, not only of the twentieth century but of all time, is not that he presided over the demise of the 'well-made play' – that was largely a coincidence – but that his contribution is fundamental and original in a way few others' have been. He is not, of course, on a par with the towering geniuses of the medium, Sophocles and Shakespeare, but is certainly comparable with the French playwright Molière and the Norwegian Henrik Ibsen. Like Molière in the seventeenth century and Ibsen in the nineteenth, he perceived instinctively the way things were going and helped them along. Such prescience involves technical innovation, certainly, but is not limited to it. That is why Beckett is greater than other influential twentieth-century dramatists such as the Italian Luigi Pirandello (1867–1936) or the German Bertolt Brecht (1898–1956), both of whom were in some respects more inventive theatrically than he was. His importance is in fact more akin to Molière's. Beckett tried to write traditional historical drama in *Human Wishes*, but found that his natural manner of writing dialogue subverted the genre so destructively and comprehensively that he had to abandon the play after a few pages. Molière did write a few traditional plays – in his case, knockabout, vulgar farces – until his own particular genius for the more serious and socially aware type of comedy (which he largely invented) asserted itself. *The Misanthrope* (1666) still retains elements of farce, but they are subordinated to the portrayal of a man who, by obstinately maintaining that total candour is not only desirable but perfectly feasible, finds himself comically at odds with a society which knows only too well that neither is the case: there would be anarchy, murder and worse if everybody spoke their minds with complete frankness. Likewise, *Waiting for Godot* has traditional elements (derived mainly from popular forms like the music-hall and the circus), but these are transcended in a play that stands, some fifty years after its first production, as the most apt dramatic image yet created of our situation in a world without God, deprived of the transcendent confidence that belief in the existence of God confers.

Having broken the mould with *Endgame* – after being trapped in it in *Human Wishes* and to a lesser extent in *Eleuthéria* – Beckett was freed of the compulsion to write full-length works. His statements could just as effectively – even more effectively – be made in tauter, tighter, more polyphonic dramatic structures. The breakthrough came with *Krapp's Last Tape*, perhaps his most perfect theatre piece. In this play, a single character is doubled, then trebled, by the use of a timely mechanical invention, the magnetic tape recorder, thus making possible a dialogue between an old man and his middle-aged earlier self, via pre-recorded tape, and their shared jokes about the young man they both once were. And the technical innovation made possible the frame that keeps painful real-life experience at the necessary emotional distance, so that few sensations are more poignant in the modern theatre than the sight of that dirty, drink-sodden old wreck listening forlornly to his earlier self asking rhetorically on the tape, 'What remains of all that misery? A girl in a shabby green coat, on a railway-station platform?' (p. 7), and offering with a bravado that conceals deeply felt regret the opinion that he was 'well out of that, Jesus yes! Hopeless business', and that he was right to break with a lover because 'it was hopeless and no good going on' (pp. 6, 10). Perfect dramatic form, beautifully crafted, and totally convincing in its effortless modernity: that is what strikes us now about *Krapp's Last Tape*.

Few critics and theatre people would therefore be surprised if Beckett is considered by posterity to rank in importance with the masters I mentioned just now, Molière and Ibsen. It is perhaps still too early to say, of course; but it *is* clear that Beckett has done as much as any dramatist in the twentieth century to extend and modify the resources of the stage, to adapt its millennial arts to the expression of the concerns and anxieties of the present age. Just as Shakespeare explored the political and moral dilemmas of the Renaissance, or Molière adjusted the anarchic world of comedy to neo-classical and rational-istic norms, or Ibsen created and transformed patterns of naturalism to give perfect expression to the psychological ghosts that stalked the European bourgeoisie in the over-confident age of imperialism and high capitalism, so Beckett has found the means of setting out the metaphysical doubts that torment us now in forms that, like all radical innovations, surprise at first and then in a short space of time begin to seem natural and inevitable. Brecht and Pirandello in the twentieth century also achieved major theatrical revolutions, as I have acknowl-edged, but it is arguable that the changes they have brought about have not been as far-reaching, nor are they likely to be as long-lasting, as those Beckett has provoked. It would be difficult to name a single important play-wright of the next generation — from Edward Albee (b.1928) to Tom Stoppard (b.1937) — be it in the British Isles, the United States, France or Germany, who has not been deeply affected by Beckett's example or influenced by his practice. Whatever posterity's verdict about his intrinsic worth and stature as a dramatist, there is no doubt that it will concede, at the very least, that he is one of the most important innovators in the history of the modern stage. This is to some extent because his con-tribution came at precisely the right moment; as another twentieth-century dramatist, John Spurling (b.1936) put it, 'Samuel Beckett was waiting for the theatre as the theatre was waiting for Samuel Beckett.'

That moment — about fifty years ago — was a moment of crisis in Modernism, the great literary and artistic movement which began in the closing years of the nine-teenth century, reached its finest flowering in the early decades of the twentieth century with such artists as Proust, Picasso and Stravinsky, and went into decline in the 1930s and 1940s. Economic and political upheaval lasting roughly from Hitler's accession to power in 1933 to the death of Stalin in 1953 forced the movement into abeyance: civilisation itself was engaged in a life-or-death struggle with the forces of inhumanity and irrationalism, and so this was no time to pursue art for art's sake. But the end of the Second World War in 1945 and humanity's gradual emergence from a nightmare world of totalitarian oppression, wholesale destruction, and killings running into many tens of millions, made it possible for Modernism to experience a second and final flowering between the 1950s and the 1970s. In this revival, known as post-modernism, Beckett played a major role, largely dictating the direction post-modern literature would take.

Modernism included, among other artistic manifestations, Symbolism, Surrealism, Cubism, Expressionism and jazz. Post-modernism, being closer to us, shows less clearly marked temporal and aesthetic contours, but it obviously includes the *nouveau roman* or 'new novel' in France, American Abstract Expressionism and pop art, electronic music, the films of such directors as Alfred Hitchcock in the United States and Ingmar Bergman in Sweden, and the so-called 'Theatre of the Absurd'. It is this theatrical phenomenon that concerns us here, since it is in the context of the contribution the stage has made to the post-modern revival that we must view Beckett's significance as a playwright; and that response has been given the convenient if somewhat restrictive label of the 'Theatre of the Absurd'. This has been defined by its leading theorist, Martin Esslin, as tending 'toward a radical devaluation of language, toward a poetry that is to emerge from the concrete and objectified images of the stage itself'; the element of language, Esslin explains, 'still plays an important part in this conception, but what *happens* on the stage transcends, and often contradicts, the *words* spoken by the characters' (*The Theatre of the Absurd*, p. 26). Esslin's point is well illustrated in a fine example of post-modern drama, Harold Pinter's play *The Homecoming* (1965), in which the banality of North London speech – 'Where's my cheese roll?' is a not untypical line from the play – masks a complex power struggle between different members of the same family which leads the wife of one of them to desert her husband and accept the role of call-girl in their employ. Likewise, the same author's first play, *The Room*, begins with chat about damp in the basement and ends with a murder and blinding of almost Sophoclean proportions; what we see in this work is a characteristically modernist shift, from metaphor in the early scenes (where one of the characters says, 'It's very cold out ... It's murder') to realism in the last episode, in which a particularly brutal killing is enacted before our very eyes. The words here, as Martin Esslin would say, are transcended by the action, and the mythic quality of the most everyday utterances brought astonishingly to life.

On the other hand, seldom has language been used more effectively in the theatre, as Dina Sherzer observes:

> Beckett is a great manipulator of, exploiter of, and performer with the manifold resources and possibilities of language. For are not the passages borrowed from other literary texts, the use of banal, everyday conversations mixed with literary language, the slang,

puns, and modified clichés, the importance granted to talking (to torment the other or to make time pass), and the careful creation of rhythms and use of repetitions all ways of demonstrating the exuberance of language and Beckett's ability to play with it and to manipulate it resulting in a new and powerful dramatic expressiveness?

(*French Review*, 1979, pp. 307–8)

In ways like these Modernism raises, for the first time in the history of drama, the issue of *meta-theatre* in an acute form. Lionel Abel has defined meta-theatre as resting upon two basic postulates: (1) that the world is a stage, and (2) that life is a dream. Neither of these two notions originated at all recently. 'Life is a dream' is the literal translation of the title of a play by the Spanish dramatist Calderón (1600–81), and 'the world's a stage' (or, in Latin, *theatrum mundi*) was a popular phrase long before Shakespeare took it up in *As You Like It*:

> All the world's a stage,
> And all the men and women merely players:
> They have their exits and their entrances;
> And one man in his time plays many parts ...
> (II. vii. 139–42)

As Elizabeth Burns comments in her book *Theatricality* (1972), 'The *theatrum mundi* metaphor was derived from the idea that God was the sole spectator of man's actions on the stage of life' (p. 143). What happened under Modernism to the venerable life-as-dream and all-the-world-a-stage metaphors was this: they were made to transcend the purely ethical plane which they occupied in the Renaissance synthesis, a sphere and context in which moral observations on the transitoriness of life, the shallowness of human endeavour, and so on, held pride of place, and men and women, as Shakespeare says, were viewed as mere actors in an absurd play, making their entrances and exits upon the stage of life and mouthing there tales 'full of sound and fury' signifying nothing. These basically religious notions were taken over by Modernism and transferred to the realm of aesthetics, where the illusory was opposed to the real, the mask to the face, the stage to the auditorium, and above all the smile was juxtaposed to the tear in that characteristically Modernist phenomenon, the wry grimace of tragicomedy. This mixed genre, which Bernard Shaw defined as being both 'deeper and grimmer' than tragedy, is indeed the Modernist mode *par excellence*. It encapsulates a great deal in the Modernist aesthetic of drama, from Ibsen's *The Wild Duck* (1884) to Beckett's *Waiting for Godot* (which is not subtitled 'a tragicomedy' for nothing).

Tragicomedy is generally considered to be marked by an air of tentativeness, but in fact what really distinguishes it is a confident stance and an assured knowingness, a knowingness shared with and by the spectator, who becomes for the first time genuinely implicated in the construction of a drama, indeed of an entire spectacle. In Ibsen's *The Wild Duck* this spectacle is that of Hjalmar's pretended 'nobility in the presence of death' which we, like one of the other characters, Dr Relling, know to be a sham, because within a year he will be holding forth with maudlin eloquence upon young Hedvig's suicide. It is also the spectacle of those clownish intellectuals in their down-at-heel togs playing histrionically to the gallery as they fill in the empty time waiting for Godot. In both cases the tone is ambiguous: Hjalmar's situation is heart-breaking, and Estragon's is desperate; but the manner in which these situations are presented is enough to make them comical. The end of Beckett's play, which has throughout balanced existential anguish against bowler-hatted slapstick straight out of the films of Laurel and Hardy, offers the ultimate in this mode. The two men have just botched an attempt at suicide: their hanging rope has snapped. Unfortunately the rope that was supposed to put an end to their sufferings also serves as the belt holding up Estragon's trousers. At one of the most sombre moments in the history of drama, at a time when all hope, even of easeful death, has evaporated: at that precise point the victim's trousers concertina around his ankles. 'Pull on your trousers,' Estragon's companion tells him. But even this is not the whole joke, because Estragon, in fine music-hall style, gets it all wrong. 'You want me to pull off my trousers?' he asks with comic oafishness. Astonishingly, we are within minutes only of the final curtain, of the unbearable poignancy of that last silence ('Let's go – *They do not move*') on which the play ends.

Beckett is one of the few dramatists to have adapted popular forms of entertainment, like the circus (the clownery of the dropped trousers) and the music-hall (Morecambe-and-Wise-type misunderstandings) in this example, to so-called 'serious' drama. His intention throughout is comic: it cannot be emphasised enough that *Waiting for Godot* is, properly performed, a very funny play. As Roger Blin, Beckett's first and greatest director, once said, 'He is unique in his ability to blend derision, humour and comedy with tragedy: his words are simultaneously tragic and comic.' There is no conflict between the circus fun of the dropping of Estragon's trousers and the intense sadness of the end of the play: in a less sophisticated way the circus, and then the masters of the silent film, Charlie Chaplin and Buster Keaton, achieved a similar balance between laughter and tears. That is what Nell means in *Endgame* when she says, in words that are cynical only in appearance, 'Nothing is funnier than unhappiness ... It's the most comical thing in the world' (p. 13). One day, in childhood, we all of us learn to laugh through our tears – 'All that matters', Beckett said once, 'is the laugh and the tear' – and in that moment we experience a great truth: to be able to laugh at our condition is the only way we can set about the necessary business of putting up with it. Beckett's great achievement is to have cast this simple intuition in the form of a witty and moving dramatic symbol: that of two clowns waiting on a country road for someone who fails to keep the appointment.

Ibsen and Beckett thus represent the poles of Modernism: in time, of course, but also in spirit; Modernism tends to be symbolic, post-modernism tends to repudiate Symbolism. That is the measure of the difficulty. How is one to define an aesthetic of modern drama that needs to embrace two such disparate figures, two giants (in their very different ways) of modern dramaturgy?

There are a few indicators, which the very 'meta-theatrical' aspect of Modernism implies. One might, for instance, attach to Modernist dramaturgy the label of 'the aesthetics of silence'. Never before had the fragmentary, the low-key, the inarticulate, even the incoherent and the frankly non-verbal tendencies of theatrical intercourse been so extensively developed. There are, of course, instances in plays dating from earlier periods of characters falling silent – aghast, amazed or terrified – but such moments remain theatrical, within the context of the play;

they do not serve as a comment upon it. The silences in Chekhov, in Pinter or in Beckett are equally justified dramatically within the play, but they also serve as a reflection upon it: in Beckett's case, quite explicitly so. 'This is deadly', comments Hamm to the audience (p. 18) when he (and we) have been exasperated by a particularly tedious piece of 'time-wasting' business from Clov. Or in *Waiting for Godot*, after the dialogue has once again run away into the sand, the characters sigh, waiting for someone to start things off once more. As embarrassed and clumsy as someone invited to a party where they know none of the other guests, Estragon is the first to break the silence through the straightforward device of simply drawing attention to it:

ESTRAGON: In the meantime nothing happens.
POZZO: You find it tedious?
ESTRAGON: Somewhat.
POZZO: (*To* VLADIMIR) And you, sir?
VLADIMIR: I've been better entertained.
   (*Silence*)

(pp. 31–2)

In spite of this tendency to lapse into wordlessness, Beckett's characters are very literate. The speakers know their classics, and quote from them liberally (Estragon from Shelley's poem 'To the Moon', Winnie of *Happy Days* – with a fine sense of irony – from *Romeo and Juliet*, while Hamm in *Endgame* sardonically distorts Baudelaire's sublime line about nightfall as the evening of his own life draws in). The inarticulacy, in other words, is in the medium as much as it is part of the message.

It is not dissimilar with Harold Pinter, who has always countered journalistic clichés about his work with the statement that he is not concerned with the so-called impossibility of communication, but rather with the fear of it; people instinctively take refuge in evasions, he believes, rather than run the risk of having to articulate what is really bothering them. Saying nothing, or talking about something irrelevant, is after all a much safer refuge than making explicit statements. The classic instance of this is the seeming irrelevance of Aston's account (in Pinter's *The Caretaker*, 1958) of his inability to drink Guinness from a thick mug whereas what really troubles him is the haunting dread of another mental breakdown, which would mean undergoing electroconvulsive therapy again. In Eugène Ionesco (1912–94), likewise, language serves rather to mask than to reveal real tensions and conflicts: *The Lesson* (1951) is a perfect exposition of how to project fantasies of rape and murder under a comically parodic form of academic discourse. But the unveiling of erotic tensions through a language to which they bear little apparent relation was certainly not invented by Ionesco: Ibsen does it superbly in *Hedda Gabler* (1890), and so do Chekhov in *Ivanov* (1887) and Strindberg in *Miss Julie* (1888). Likewise, Pinter is not the first playwright to show characters evading a realisation of their plight: Chekhov's Gayev takes refuge from his embarrassments in *The Cherry Orchard* (1904) by imagining himself playing billiards, 'potting into the corner pocket', as he exclaims, or 'cannoning off the cushions'. The spectacle of language breaking down, the explosion of the hysteria underlying the polite banalities of social intercourse, and violence resulting from quite trivial provocations: all this forms the basis of Chekhov's drama, just as it does of Pinter's. There is a marked difference in setting, of course: the estates of the declining nobility in pre-revolutionary Russia are a far cry from the seedy bed-and-breakfasts or the trendy modernised farmhouses in which Harold Pinter's characters, from *The Birthday Party* (1957) to *Old Times* (1971), tear each other apart, but both are the authentic locales of their respective periods. Long after the last derelict London mansion has been erased by the developer's JCBs as irrevocably as Madame Ranyevskaia's cherry orchard has been cut down by its new owner's axemen, Pinter's people, like Chekhov's, will still be probing the resources of speech in order to find loopholes through which to escape from their truths, signalling as they go messages of hostility and repressed antagonism, either by the use of inappropriate discourse (like Mick's assertion to the tramp Davies in *The Caretaker*, 1958, 'I understood you were an experienced first-class professional interior and exterior decorator ... You mean you wouldn't know how to fit teal-blue, copper and parchment linoleum squares and have those colours re-echoed in the walls? ... You're a bloody impostor, mate!'), or by non-verbal means, as when in the same play the Buddha statue is smashed against the gas stove.

In pursuing further this theme of meta-theatre as the one possible unifying characteristic of Modernist drama, one cannot fail to note the 'life is a dream' motif that runs through so much of it. Central to the theatre of Luigi Pirandello (1867–1936) is the ambiguous interaction of the 'fictive' and the 'real', but this derives in its turn from Strindberg's *Dream Play* (1901), a work of profound and revolutionary originality, and leads on afterwards to one of the most perfect works thrown up in the post-1950 rebirth of Modernism, *Professor*

*Taranne* (1951) by Arthur Adamov, in which an eminent academic finds himself accused of a list of offences of ever-increasing gravity, ranging from lack of courtesy towards colleagues and students, to plagiarising the work of another scholar, and finally to indecent exposure. It is impossible to be sure, within the terms set by the play itself, whether or not the professor is the victim of a concerted campaign of defamation and distortion, or genuinely guilty of the offences alleged against him. When, on being told the contents of the Belgian vice-chancellor's letter explaining why his invitation to come and give lectures is not being renewed, Professor Taranne slowly starts taking his clothes off as the curtain falls, the audience is unsure if he is merely conforming to the nightmare, or confirming its truth. The success of this play lies in the fact that its ambiguity remains entire: is Taranne's professorial demeanour a mask for paranoia and deviant behaviour? What is the reality, and what the illusion? These are questions that Modernism is adept at posing, undermining our categories and destroying our confidence in familiar things and places: such as a middle-class flat, a safe enough place, one would have thought, until Eugène Ionesco in *Amédée* (1954) peopled it with an expanding corpse and covered its carpets with mushrooms, or until Harold Pinter in *The Room* made it the scene of the Sophoclean ritual murder and blinding I referred to earlier. Life is here implicated with art, and art with life: when tragedies are enacted in the drawing room, when – as in Pinter's *The Homecoming* – Iphigenia is sacrificed in North London, or when Shakespeare's *The Taming of the Shrew* is rewritten by Edward Albee as *Who's Afraid of Virginia Woolf?* (1962), we return by another route to that essential tragicomedy which, as we have seen, is so inseparable from Modernism.

Equally characteristic is an attitude to the theatrical space that either divides it somewhere across the middle, or throws the barrier around the playhouse altogether. Drama before Modernism sought to foster the illusion that the audience was eavesdropping, that a 'fourth wall' had fallen away unbeknown to the characters and that the spectators were looking straight in. Ibsen does not disdain this trick, since trick is what it is: *The Wild Duck* begins in the most conventional manner imaginable, with the family servant explaining to the hired waiter the situation from which the drama is to spring (similar to what, in classical theatre, was known as the exposition, a function normally carried out in the prologue). It is a rather obvious device, since Ibsen has engineered, by this simple artifice, for the audience to be 'put in the picture' and the action started. This awkward but essential phase once past, the play is performed just as if an audience were not watching; indeed, it needs to be so performed if dramatic tension is going to be effectively created. The actors have to concentrate hard on the situation; any hint of a gesture to the gallery would destroy the illusion.

Yet it is precisely this illusion – the illusion of realist drama, epitomised by the juxtaposition of a darkened, hushed auditorium and a brightly lit, busy stage – that Bertolt Brecht sought to abolish. This did not entail removing the footlights and making the stage and auditorium continuous. On the contrary: to do that would have been to create another illusion, just as totalitarian, that the world *within* the theatre walls is a real world, the only genuine one, an illusion which theorists such as Antonin Artaud (1896–1948) and playwrights such as Jean Genet

(1910–86) strove to promulgate in their work. As a Marxist, Brecht was the exact opposite of mystics like Artaud and visionaries like Genet: his rejection of realistic illusion had a didactic and political purpose, but his innovations have opened up the way to much else that is vital in contemporary theatre, not least the works of Samuel Beckett, which self-consciously play 'across' the footlights. In *Waiting for Godot* the emptiness of the auditorium is humorously commented upon by the actor/characters; in *Endgame*, Hamm – like the 'ham' actor (meaning an actor of indifferent talent) that he is – plays to the gallery, and when Clov asks what it is that keeps them there, replies, truthfully enough, 'the dialogue' (p. 35); and in *Happy Days*, Winnie 'begins her day' like an old trouper, aroused by the peremptory bell summoning her like a stage-hand rapping on her dressing-room door, limbering up for another run through the familiar material. Likewise, Ionesco never tires of reminding the audience that they are sitting in a playhouse, watching a game the rules of which may be modified but still need to be respected; in such stage-discussions Ionesco is not above puckishly referring to himself by name.

It is clear that these and other features can, in default of a single and consistent aesthetic, be seen as helping to make up the Modernist synthesis. Some of the other features (ritual and fairy tale, mask and dance, stylisation and formalisation, relativity and flux), though equally important, need not detain us: they all derive essentially from the major traits that I have identified. Many of these aspects can, naturally enough, be observed operating in parallel in other performing arts in this century, such as the ballet, the cinema or, more recently, television.

To summarise, the principal characteristics of drama since Ibsen and Chekhov can be enumerated as follows:

1 A tone of 'serious levity' towards drama, and particularly towards the classics of the medium, as we saw in Edward Albee's reworking of Shakespeare's *Taming of the Shrew* in his play *Who's Afraid of Virginia Woolf?*, and which can also be found in Tom Stoppard's post-modern revision of *Hamlet*, first performed in 1967, *Rosencrantz and Guildenstern Are Dead*.

2 The exploration of antagonism and violence, particularly of a psychological kind, in the shadow of what Stoppard has called 'the great homicidal classics' (chief among which, of course, is *Hamlet*: as Stoppard points out, it is 'a slaughterhouse', accounting for 'eight corpses all told' by the end).

3 'Meta-theatre' (founded, as we saw, on two basic postulates, one, that the world is a stage, and two, that life is a dream), signifying a medium totally aware of itself and involving the spectator in an equally searching act of self-awareness.

4 A preference for the mixed genre of tragicomedy rather than the 'purer' forms favoured by classical theatre, tragedy or comedy.

5 A movement – sponsored particularly by Brecht – away from the 'picture-frame' stage towards a tendency to play 'across' the footlights.

If all this seems confusing, it is because modern drama since 1900 has been one of the most bewilderingly lively and inventive of European art forms. There is no simple pattern, but rather a tension, a continual dialectic. The twin forces pulling in different directions in Beckett's theatre – those of rigour on the one hand, and of feeling on the other – are a case in point. It is such interaction, not only within modern drama, but also between contemporary plays and the classics of the past, that makes the theatre of the latter half of the twentieth century in general, and its leading exponent Beckett in particular, such a fascinating object of study. This book aims at giving you every possible help and assistance in that quest.

## Beckett's Dramatic Development

In a writing career spanning six decades, from the early 1930s to the late 1980s, it is not surprising that Beckett developed considerably as a dramatist over those years. His evolution can be traced in six broad phases (see also the Chronology, pp. 147–8). The first represents the apprentice years during the 1930s, in which he wrote a college sketch (*Le Kid*, a parody of Corneille's drama of 1636, *Le Cid*) and began the ambitious four-act play *Human Wishes*, about the relationship between the great English writer Dr Johnson and his benefactress Mrs Thrale, of which only part of one scene was ever completed. Then came the forced interruption of the war years (1939–45), immediately after which Beckett wrote two full-length plays, *Eleuthéria* (still unperformed) and *Waiting for Godot*. These represent his second phase, in which he was finding his own distinctive voice as a playwright; neither work, however, is fully mature as first written. *Eleuthéria* Beckett was content to abandon once it became clear that *Godot*, with only five characters as opposed to over three times that number, would be cheaper and easier to put on than the first play. *Waiting for*

*Godot* than developed considerably in production. The differences between the first published text in French (1952), and the version Beckett used in productions in which he himself later became involved, are considerable; as James Knowlson's monumental edition of the theatrical notebooks (see Select Bibliography, p. 149) makes clear, the current text is both shorter and tauter, much more an acting script, than the often rather self-indulgently literary version that a less experienced playwright handed to his publisher shortly after it was written. The remarkable thing is the originality of the basic conception, which Beckett needed only to refine and sharpen over the years; even if he was not always sure about details, and allowed the circumstances of individual productions to dictate minor variations from the basic scheme he laid down in the notebooks, he never had any doubts or hesitations about the essential shape and thrust of the play.

For several years after completing *Waiting for Godot* he abandoned writing for the stage and spent much time instead translating his French works into English. But the notoriety of that play put pressure on him to write another. The BBC suggested that he try his hand at radio drama, then a flourishing medium (this was the period immediately following the publication of Dylan Thomas's verse masterpiece for radio, *Under Milk Wood*, 1954), and *All That Fall* (1957) was the result. At the same time Beckett was struggling with another stage-play, and finally produced *Endgame*. These two works, plus the *Acts Without Words*, the 'roughs' or fragments for theatre, and *Krapp's Last Tape*, constitute, in the late 1950s, a third phase.

*All That Fall* was for Beckett a new departure, in that he moved into a different medium, radio; but in itself it is a relatively traditional work with a naturalistic setting and everyday characters. *Endgame*, on the other hand, was a radically experimental work by any standard. The claustrophobic set, the terminal situation and the characters without identifiable origins that all characterise *Endgame* made *Waiting for Godot* seem a work almost of social realism in comparison (it tells us something, after all, about tramps' preferences in root vegetables, not to mention the problems they have with footwear). The harsh and unremitting nature of *Endgame*, its refusal to make any concessions to the audience's hunger for progression or development of the situation on stage, link it with the remorseless monologues in the novel *The Unnamable* (1953) and in the *Texts for Nothing* (1955), whereas, as Beckett himself suggested, the tone of *Waiting for Godot* is closer to that of the pre-war novel *Murphy* (1938). *Krapp's Last Tape* is equally radical, a mono-drama in which the characters are reduced to one, an old man communing with an earlier self via the tape recorder that brings back voices from his past. Although at first sight the dramatic situation appears dangerously com-pressed, the play succeeds brilliantly in conveying the agonising poignancy of Krapp's loss. No spectator who has seen a competent production (and the play, as we shall see, is technically quite difficult to stage) can ever forget the intense emotion felt when decrepit old Krapp listens helplessly to his middle-aged predecessor waxing lyrical about 'the fire in me now' (p. 13), a fire that, all too obviously, was long ago extinguished in the decayed geriatric we see before us.

A fourth phase opens in 1959 with *Embers*, a radio play as radical in conception as *All That Fall* is traditional. This time Beckett seizes on the fact that the origin of a sound on the radio is essentially ambiguous and uncertain: is it meant to be live, recorded, or merely imaginary? Is it inside the protagonist's head or has it some independent source? In the other radio plays of this period Beckett exploited this discovery to the full, and indeed worked it through so that, after *Cascando* (1963), he found no further challenge in this medium. He was already moving into film (with *Film*, 1965) and television (with *Eh Joe*, 1966). Indeed, he quickly discovered a particular affinity with the intimate, small-scale possibilities of television, the reduced décors, the limited number of actors, the concentration and informality of the small screen, and above all the feasibility of using the camera as a character in its own right. He was encouraged in this new interest by the television service in southern Germany, Süddeutscher Rundfunk (SDR), Stuttgart, which invited him to direct *Eh Joe* himself, in German translation; the resulting production was in fact transmitted by SDR before the BBC, for whom it was written, got the English-language version on the air. Beckett returned several times to Stuttgart after that to direct works for television which he had written with this enlightened patron specifically in mind.

But this phase was equally rich in stage-plays of great originality. From *Happy Days* (1961), through *Play* (1963) and *Come and Go* (1966) to *Breath* (1969), Beckett continually invented new ways of using the theatrical space. In *Happy Days* the protagonist is imprisoned in the earth surrounded by her meagre possessions, and is forced to act, to play, by the peremptory ringing of a harsh bell. 'Begin your day, Winnie,' she tells herself (p. 138), and gallantly takes up the challenge like the seasoned old pro that she is. In *Play*, three individuals, barely recognisable as human beings, retell at the behest of an inquisitorial beam of light as domineering as Winnie's bell a sadly comic tale of adultery. The innovation here is to have them repeat the play they have just run through so that two acts, as it were, are squeezed out of one. *Come and Go* and *Breath* reduced drama to the briefest statement possible; *Breath*, in particular, is just that, an inhalation and an exhalation heard as an amplified recording on a stage empty of everything except rubbish.

Many thought that Beckett had written his last play in *Breath*, seen in 1969 as the culmination of his entire development as a dramatist to that date. They were wrong. He did not write another play for some years, admittedly, spending much time in the late 1960s directing his own plays in Paris and Berlin. But a fifth phase began in 1972 with *Not I*, a punishingly difficult work for an actress to perform, since her delivery must be carefully articulated but so rapid as to be barely comprehensible. Then followed two further explorations of extreme theatre, *That Time* (1976), with nothing but a lit face and three monologues pre-recorded by the same actor, and *Footfalls*, with low, slow voices conducting a ghostly dialogue as an old woman shuffles to and fro. Two further and even more reduced experiments in television, *Ghost Trio* and ... *but the clouds* ..., belong to this phase of the mid-1970s.

The sixth phase began in 1979 after another busy interval of self-direction with theatre companies in London, Paris and Berlin. All the dramatic works of the last period of Beckett's life are short, even 'occasional', in the sense of having been written for a specific event, such as a benefit night for a persecuted fellow playwright, or conceived for a particular actor whose work had impressed Beckett. Thus *Catastrophe* was written in 1982 to support the Czech dissident Vaclav Havel, and *A Piece of Monologue* (1979) for David Warrilow to perform. Slight as some of these late works are, they have their moments of dramatic intensity, and they all show that even in old age Beckett remained theatrically as inventive and unpredictable as ever. In his last play, *What Where* (1984), the penultimate sentence, 'Make sense who may', provoked many spectators to sigh, 'Yes, indeed', which was perhaps what had all along been the intention of our frequently jocular, sometimes teasing, author.

## Performance and Response

It all began not (as one might expect) with *Waiting for Godot*'s crucial opening on 5 January 1953, but with the piece of juvenilia I have already mentioned. This was a college parody staged anonymously long before *Waiting for Godot*: between 19 and 21 February 1931, in fact, when the Peacock Theatre in Dublin saw the first (and last) performances of Beckett's earliest dramatic work, *Le Kid*, written in collaboration with a life-long friend Georges Pelorson, at that time a French-exchange lector at Trinity College, Dublin. Apart from giving rise to a laconic review in the student newspaper, this début made few ripples, although the critical reaction to the unveiling of a new work by a novice playwright does not differ markedly from others I shall be discussing. As the next play, *Human Wishes*, never got beyond the first scene, and the one after that, *Eleuthéria*, remains unperformed, we jump more than twenty years to the saga of the staging of *Waiting for Godot*.

Beckett wrote *Waiting for Godot* rapidly, in the winter

of 1948 to 1949, between the novels *Malone Dies* and *The Unnamable*, and on this occasion he naturally aimed at something more professional than a college production. It happened (the way these things often do, more or less by chance) that at the time Roger Blin, who had been a friend of the great theorist I have already mentioned, Antonin Artaud, and had acted in one of his experimental works before the war, was putting on Strindberg's *Ghost Sonata* at a small Left Bank theatre in Paris, and Beckett went to see it. Thinking that Blin was the ideal person to stage his own play, he sent him the typescript. When he had overcome Beckett's shyness sufficiently to allow them to meet, Blin was curious to know why he had been chosen. Because he was faithful to Strindberg, to both the letter and the spirit, and because the theatre was nearly empty, was the reply. Beckett felt sure – Blin was later to relate – that his own text would therefore be respected and that the theatre would be empty, which seemed to the novice playwright the ideal condition for a good performance.

Undeterred by the eccentricity of this view, Blin was won over by the play, but it took him another three years to put it on. A small government grant enabled him, early in 1953, to stage the play at another small Paris theatre, the Théâtre Babylone; and the rest, as they say, is history. Press reaction was predictably mixed, but what counted were the reactions of fellow-writers, which were uniformly enthusiastic. The great French playwright Jean Anouilh (1910–87) did not beat about the bush: the opening of *Waiting for Godot*, he asserted, was as significant as the first staging, in Paris forty years earlier, of a Pirandello play; and he was telling the simple truth – Pirandello's impact on the dramaturgy of the inter-war years was on much the same scale as Beckett's has been in the last few decades. The influential avant-garde novelist Alain Robbe-Grillet (b.1922) perceptively credited Roger Blin with emphasising the 'circus aspects' of the play and thus contributing materially to its success. Blin is in fact one of the few directors to have influenced Beckett: it was at Blin's instigation that he cut several passages which seemed too long or literary, or which broke the tension in some way. This explains why the second French edition, which appeared after the Babylone première, differs from the first of 1952, and why the English translation, carried out by Beckett himself and published in 1954, shows extensive deletions. A measure of his gratitude to Blin for giving him confidence as a playwright is shown by the dedication of *Endgame* to his first director, whose basic approach to *Waiting for Godot* has broadly been accepted as definitive. The play on whch Blin so indelibly left his mark has established itself as an uncontested classic of the French stage: almost like Racine's tragedies, one critic half-jokingly remarked, it has become one of the pillars of the nation's theatre, a remarkable feat for an author who was not even born in France.

The fortunes of *Waiting for Godot* elsewhere in the world have been, if anything, still more brilliant. It was seen in Warsaw, then part of the Soviet system, even before it was staged in London, where it ran first at the Arts Theatre then at the Criterion from August 1955 to the following May. Despite this success, the London production was preceded by the same rather sordid material difficulties as the Paris creation had been, and the New York staging was also. The Earl of Harewood wished to put it on, but had to give up the project through lack of funds. The next idea was for Peter Glenville to direct the world-famous actors Ralph Richardson in the role of Estragon and Alec Guinness in that of Vladimir, but Richardson's initial enthusiasm for the part was dampened by Beckett's failure to offer him any elucidation as to what Pozzo represents, so, on finding that Beckett could not (or would not) 'explain' the play to him, he let the part go, only to regret his decision later. In this he was quite unlike the even more famous British actor John Gielgud, who when later approached about *Endgame* turned it down because he 'couldn't stand it or understand it' (*Sunday Times*, 24 September 1961). In fact, apart from Bert Lahr, America's first Estragon, and Madeleine Renaud, the first French Winnie in *Happy Days*, few prominent stars or famous performers have managed to accommodate their style to Beckett's plays: these have, on the whole, been much better served by initially less well known but more flexible actors such as Jack MacGowran or Billie Whitelaw. Such performers, in common with the directors for whom they worked, were able to accept that a play may have a poetic meaning which cannot be summarised in a few sentences and which, in any case, only emerges in a performance that seeks as faithfully as possible to follow the author's instructions and leave the overtones to take care of themselves. It was probably better for the play, in fact, that Richardson did not in the end take the part of Estragon: he would undoubtedly have given a fine performance, but it would have been very much a *performance*, not unlike that offered by Madeleine Renaud as Winnie, rather than the more effective playing of, say, Alfred Lynch, who was all the more eloquent in the role of Estragon in a new staging of the play in 1964 because he was less famous, more self-effacing, and allowed the character to come alive through him.

*Waiting for Godot* eventually fell in the way of a little-known young man Peter Hall (now the much better known Sir Peter Hall), who became its first British director. His Pozzo, Peter Bull, suffered acute discomfort from the bald wig he was required by the part to wear and, since he found so many of the cues identical, tended to leave out whole chunks of the play. In other ways, too, Hall's production was far from perfect: it over-stressed the tramps aspect, going beyond Beckett's spare stage-directions by adding a dustbin and miscellaneous rubbish to the required tree, and gave correspondingly less weight to the clownish elements which later productions, not least Beckett's own, have tended to highlight instead. Perhaps not surprisingly, the London daily papers treated the first night with bafflement and derision, but the following Sunday the influential drama critic Harold Hobson published one of the most moving and perceptive notices of his entire distinguished career in the play's defence. This turned the tide, and *Waiting for Godot* has never failed to attract British audiences since.

Early in 1956, Faber and Faber, who had managed to acquire the British publication rights despite some initial hesitations, published Beckett's English translation of the play. This was reviewed in the cultural establishment's weekly broadsheet, the *Times Literary Supplement*, by a leading critic, G. S. Fraser, who claimed that the play 'extracts from the *idea* of boredom the most genuine pathos and enchanting comedy'. He went on to remark that it is 'essentially a prolonged and sustained metaphor about the nature of human life', and this unassuming exegesis triggered off a correspondence with the editor about the 'meaning' of the play which continued for several weeks and in which the great critic and poet

William Empson, among others, took part. After publishing six of his readers' letters the editor closed this very British exchange by singling out for special praise a correspondent who had suggested that Vladimir represents the soul, Estragon the body, and Pozzo and Lucky damnation; and he expressed the hope that the author himself would write to the paper and clear up the mystery. Needless to say, Beckett did no such thing, which is perhaps not so surprising in view of the discovery (made by one of his fictional characters, Molloy) that the *Times Literary Supplement* serves admirably as a makeshift blanket since 'even farts made no impression on its never-failing toughness and impermeability' (*The Novels*, p. 30).

London's next major production of *Waiting for Godot*, Alan Simpson's with an Irish cast from Dublin, prompted the great socio-literary critic Raymond Williams (1921–88), in his review in the *New Statesman* (19 May 1961), to stress Beckett's 'very powerful dramatic imagery, of a virtually universal kind'. With characteristic perceptiveness, Williams took the opportunity to draw attention to the play's basic, 'quite formal' structure, and to the fact that 'because of its flexibility and subtlety, even its deep ambiguity of tone, it is a play that requires an emotionally educated audience'. The BBC, which had already done something to educate that audience with *All That Fall* in 1957, continued the good work by broadcasting *Waiting for Godot* on television in 1961 and on radio as part of a series, 'From the Fifties', in 1962. When the play was revived at the Royal Court Theatre late in 1964 there was little difficulty about the audience, which 'clapped and clapped and went on clapping', according to the *Daily Telegraph* reviewer. This production by Anthony Page, supervised this time by Beckett himself, had the kind of authoritativeness shown in the Paris Odéon staging of 1961. The press this time was uniformly favourable. 'I admit it,' confessed Bernard Levin in the *Daily Mail*, 'Mr Hobson was right'; not all the tucking into humble pie was as forthright as this, but the general tenor was the same. Reviewers even wondered what all the fuss had been about nine years previously: the play, they roundly asserted, was not in the least obscure, but had the limpid simplicity of a great classic. On the eve of opening, the *Daily Mail* indulged in a facetious Christmassy note: 'a stone's throw from the citadels of panto, Lucky makes his bow, but it's a far cry from Mother Goose', because now nobody was afraid of the big bad wolf any more. With characteristic modesty, Harold Hobson refrained from crowing 'I told you so,' but he did just allow himself this aside: '*Waiting for Godot* – we all know it now – is a very great play' (*Sunday Times*, 17 January 1965). For the rest of his notice he bestowed glowing (and fully merited) praise on Nicol Williamson's performance as Vladimir and 'his jaunty Scots accent, his sudden bursts of gaiety, his agilely shambling half-run, half-walk, his confident assertions followed immediately by doubts and qualifications, his innumerable suggestions for games and diversions, his brief but total collapses'. In such moments Williamson stood 'absolutely forlorn in broken bowler and ragged trousers, nothing moving except his sad, distressed eyes ...' There was equal praise for Jack MacGowran in the part of Lucky ('he has acted himself so far into Beckett's mind he almost seems part of its imagery' wrote the *New Statesman*'s critic), and so well did he, Paul Curran (as Pozzo) and Alfred Lynch (as Estragon) serve their roles that a newcomer to the play might have been forgiven for assuming it had been written specially for them. They were given credit by reviewers for achieving the far from easy feat of establishing clear differences between the characters: Estragon came over suitably 'morose', Pozzo 'hectoring', Lucky 'doleful' and Vladimir 'restless'.

By this time the battle over Beckett's status as a dramatist had moved from newspaper offices to university campuses, where student directors and actors took him up enthusiastically, and professors like myself began turning the spotlight of their critical scholarship on the most obscure corners of his collected writings, with, as one might expect, unequal results. Some academics, such as the American Hugh Kenner and the Frenchman Jean-Jacques Mayoux, have left an indelible mark on Beckett studies (as they soon came to be called: by 1976 there was even a *Journal of Beckett Studies* adorning library shelves, a fact which gave wry amusement to its much-studied subject); but other learned responses were less felicitous. In his review of one scholarly tome, the leading playwright John Mortimer singled out for scornful rebuttal a claim that what Vladimir and Estragon do is of no importance: on the contrary, replied Mortimer, 'what Vladimir and Estragon do is of supreme importance, demonstrated by the minute and beautiful care with which the play is contrived'. The professor's well-meant but misguided attempts to 'disregard the actual incidents of a play and apprehend instead the general theme of the author' fell foul, Mortimer argued, of the reality that in the work of an 'undoubted genius' like Beckett there is 'total lack of a general theme', merely 'an intense and painful individual expression'. Playwrights in general have, perhaps not surprisingly, been far more perceptive than most academics in discerning the precise nature of

Beckett's theatrical achievement: the American dramatist Thornton Wilder considered *Waiting for Godot* one of the greatest modern plays, and the Spanish playwright Alfonso Sastre maintained that 'while we are left cold by many dramas of intrigue in which a great deal happens, this "nothing happens" of *Waiting for Godot* keeps us in suspense'. As for writers of the following generation, we have seen that Harold Pinter and Tom Stoppard, for example, owe him a great debt.

The all-pervading influence of Beckett's language and imagery is nowhere more tellingly revealed than in the uses political cartoonists have put them to. During the last days of the Conservative government in 1964, the great left-wing satirist Vicky (Victor Weisz, 1913–66) was inspired to depict Prime Minister Harold Macmillan as Vladimir and one of his Cabinet colleagues as Estragon ruefully contemplating newspaper headlines about 'Budget Hopes' and declaring, 'We'll hang ourselves tomorrow ... Unless Godot comes.' Truly, as the critic Ronald Bryden saw in 1965, Beckett had 'become a climate of opinion'; his clowns had not only tramped all over the globe, they had become part of twentieth-century mythology.

After such an apotheosis, it was perhaps only to be expected that the creation of *Endgame* (the work that gave rise to such critical clichés of the time as 'dustbin philosophy' and 'ashcan drama') would turn out to be something of an anti-climax. As we shall see, Beckett had begun thinking about writing a new play in 1954, but only started work on it in December 1955. At first it consisted of two acts, but since it soon became clear to Beckett that there was no aesthetic justification for a binary structure as there had been in *Waiting for Godot*, in revising his first typescript Beckett removed the interval and cut out other unsatisfactory material to leave the longish one-act play we are familiar with. It gave him far more trouble than *Waiting for Godot*: not until October 1956 was Roger Blin able to begin rehearsals, once again without immediate hope of finding a theatre in which to put it on.

In the end, since no Paris house could be persuaded to risk it, Blin accepted the Royal Court's invitation to première *Endgame* in London on 3 April 1957. Though I was a hard-up student at the time, I was determined to be there, and was privileged to watch Roger Blin create the role of Hamm and Jean Martin that of Clov, but I have to admit, nearly half a century later, that the well-intentioned compromise of performing a new and difficult French play in London was not a success; Beckett described the occasion to another theatre person soon afterwards as 'rather grim, like playing to mahogany, or rather teak'. The fault cannot, however, be said to lie entirely with an audience which of necessity did not fully understand the language the actors were speaking; the production itself must bear part of the responsibility for the semi-fiasco, being rather monotonous, shrill and disjointed. Jacques Noel's décor consisted of an over-literal grey-green cave-like interior which added to the oppressive effect. Clearly the actors were not at ease at the Royal Court, nor in their roles: a kind of sullen resentment seemed to flow back and forth across the footlights, and even such a sympathetic reviewer as Georges Pelorson regretted a certain slowness and forced quality in Blin's delivery. When the production transferred to the Studio des Champs-Élysées on 26 April the Paris critics received the play with respect on the whole, but with little enthusiasm, and Beckett's old friend of Trinity days, A. J. Leventhal, had to concede in the *Dublin Magazine* that '*Endgame* cannot hope for the same success that attended *Waiting for Godot* ... an audience, faced with uttermost pain on the stage, is likely to wilt at the experience, though it may well be a catharsis for such who have hitherto refused in their euphoria to look beyond the end of their optimistic noses.'

In Beckett's English translation this time, *Endgame* returned to London and to the Royal Court on 28 October 1958 in a double bill with *Krapp's Last Tape*. The director was an old friend of Beckett's, George Devine, and he played Hamm; Jack MacGowran took the part of Clov and made it one of his greatest roles. Critics reacted with distaste or with facetiousness, but Roy Walker sprang to the play's defence, arguing in *The Twentieth Century* that Beckett cannot be written off as a 'unique pathological oddity'; his 'scathing satires on the sin and instability of man' must be seen as ranking 'among the greatest plays yet to appear upon the modern stage', for 'he has found in the depths of despair "the right kind of pity" for the individual and universal condition of our time'. Walker drew attention to Shakespearean overtones in *Endgame* (Hamm being a cross between Prospero and Richard III), but the most thoroughgoing exploration of this particular theme was a controversial essay entitled '*King Lear*, or Endgame' by the influential Polish critic Jan Kott: 'in both Shakespearean and Beckettian Endgames it is the modern world that fell; the Renaissance world, and ours'. Modish as Kott's views tended to be, they had the merit, in treating Shakespeare's plays as savage parables for our own age, of illuminating several parallels of mood and theme between them and Beckett's, suggesting incidentally that the latter may, of all twentieth-century playwrights, be the one who approaches nearest to Shakespearean universality and poetic directness.

*Endgame* was next seen in a major production in London in July 1964. Starring Patrick Magee (for whom, it will be remembered, *Krapp's Last Tape* was written) in the role of Hamm, and Jack MacGowran once again as Clov, it had already enjoyed a successful run in Paris (in English). Once again, too, Beckett took a hand in the direction, and reviewers were not slow to notice that in contrast to Blin's rather frigid, even humourless version, it revealed a bawdy, coarse robustness which made the whole livelier and more interesting dramatically. Critics were unanimous in their praise for the Magee–MacGowran duo: 'they are consistently alert to each other's moods and project a relationship which is a mixture of reluctant affection and animosity, desperation and sullen dependence', wrote Peter Lennon in the *Guardian*. Their interpretation was as near to definitive as those in the 1964 audience were likely to see. *Endgame*, as Beckett himself recognised, is a difficult play to get right. So perhaps the initial critical resistance to the work was due in part to production teething troubles; or perhaps it is quite simply easier for us to take the play now. 'A masterpiece of ambiguity' in the view of the Australian academic Ross Chambers, deliberately less rich and more spare than *Waiting for Godot*, *Endgame* is arguably a greater achievement, with its Shakespearean and Strindbergian dimensions (there could well be, in the choice of setting, a conscious reminiscence of the fortress in Strindberg's *Dance of Death*).

Beckett's next stage play, *Krapp's Last Tape*, was, unlike *Endgame*, recognised straightaway as a dramatic masterpiece. Beckett had been impressed by Patrick Magee reading extracts (in a truly unforgettable rasping voice) from his novels on BBC radio in the late 1950s, and wrote the play, and designed the part of Krapp, with him specifically in mind. The Irish actor duly created the role under Donald McWhinnie's direction as the curtain-raiser in the 1958 double bill with *Endgame* mentioned earlier. In the review already cited, Roy Walker confidently predicted that 'future histories of the drama' would 'have something to say' about *Krapp's Last Tape*, a play in which a character engages in dialogue with a person present on stage, though not in the flesh, but rather recorded on tape. 'Flawless', 'economical', 'haunting' and 'harrowing' were some of the laudatory epithets heaped on the production by critics, one of whom went so far as to call it a 'lyrical poem of solitude'. But as with other works, audiences had to wait for something near to a definitive interpretation until the author was able to become more closely involved. This occurred in 1969 at Berlin's Schiller Theater, with Martin Held starring as Krapp, in a production directed by Beckett which has come to represent a sort of benchmark for later actors as they prepare their own performance in the role.

## Problems of Interpretation

As we saw, when *Waiting for Godot* was first put on in London, a flurry of articles and letters to editors attempted to answer the question: 'What does the play mean?' It is now quite clear, after the passage of nearly half a century, that the answer is simply, as Beckett said at the time, 'It means what it says.' There are two main reasons for this. Firstly, none of the 'interpretations' offered, Christian or otherwise, fitted all the facts, and most were obliged, in order to put forward a coherent view, to ignore passages which did not square with that reading. Secondly, Beckett's other works have become more widely known since 1955, and they show clearly that he is not a didactic author concerned to put across a 'message' in literary form. Such 'truths' as he does enunciate are simple observations about the human condition that have been common coin since Job and Sophocles. It is an undeniable fact, for instance, that, as a life-assurance tycoon put it recently with impressive candour, we all, sooner or later, are going to die, and many people today are doubtful whether anything lies beyond death. Beckett's works are not, however, *statements* of this theme, but *meditations* upon it, and early critics mistook the latter for the former. They were, it is true, misled to some extent by the Christian echoes that abound in *Waiting for Godot*. For example, when Vladimir asks, 'We are not saints, but we have kept our appointment; how many people can boast as much?' (p. 72), spectators who know their Bible can answer, 'the Wise Virgins' (see Matthew 24: 25). Some writers, such as William Golding (1911–93), might incorporate an allusion like that into a complex but coherent religious statement. Not so Beckett. The reason for the presence of Christian elements in his works is simple: 'Christianity', he once said to an enquirer, 'is a mythology with which I am familiar, so I naturally use it.' In other words, he is interested in mythologies for their own sake, without any commitment to them whatsoever. As he put it to another interviewer, 'I'm not interested in any system. I can't see any trace of any system anywhere.'

Beckett is, in truth, the complete agnostic: he is simply not interested in whether the Christian Church is telling fairy stories or not. Even were God to exist, the fact of his existence would not, according to Beckett, make any difference: he would be as lonely and as enslaved as the voice in *The Unnamable*, and as isolated and ridiculous as humankind is, in a cold, silent, indifferent universe. If *Waiting for Godot* can be called religious at all, it is a poem about a world without any divinity but a kind of malignant fate, a world in which human beings wait and hope for something, anything, to give meaning to their lives and relieve them of the absurdity of a death which, as far as they are concerned, puts an irrevocable end to everything they have ever felt and experienced. But they wait in vain, and so our life is as meaningless as our death. Between a human being's life and a mayfly's there is, in the last analysis, little to choose; hence Pozzo's remark, 'the light gleams an instant' (p. 82), an instant only. It is, after all, a monstrous paradox that, for the individual, life is an eternity while it lasts, but that it is less than an instant with regard to cosmic time, just as a person's five or six feet in height is nothing compared with the immense distances separating the galaxies. Human consciousness, of course, is all, but the consciousness by which people are aware of their individual existence is continually at risk from bodily failure or mental breakdown.

Humankind is in any case held in a two-dimensional prison: time. In this prison, only forward motion is possible, but humanity deludes itself that it is progressing of its own free will to some sort of goal. As Beckett put it in *Proust* (1931), 'We are rather in the position of Tantalus, with this difference, that we allow ourselves to be tantalised'; little wonder, then, that 'We are disappointed at the nullity of what we are pleased to call attainment' (p. 3). In Beckett's best-known play, that nullity is called 'Godot'. Birth is a 'calamity' because it launches us on our one-dimensional way (see the discussion about repentance for 'being born', p. 3), and the only release from that is death. *Waiting for Godot* is therefore, put simply, a portrayal of the antics of humankind as it tries to distract itself until 'Godot' comes. But Godot is only death. He is not, however, seen as death, because we flatter ourselves with groundless hopes; thus Godot becomes anything the expectation of which helps us to bear our existence. Or as Estragon puts it, 'We always find something, eh Didi, to give us the impression we exist?' (p. 61).

It is therefore evident that a Christian interpretation, which would see some hope of salvation, in spite of all, in the arrival of Pozzo or the boy messenger, is as unhelpful as a Marxist reading, which would see the play as an indictment of the alienation of people under capitalism. Both these and other exegeses – even those that see it as a manifesto for atheism – make the mistake of assuming that a work of the imagination must have a *positive* meaning, whereas this one avoids the positive and the definite like the plague. It operates exclusively by hint and understatement; it has, in fact, been most aptly termed 'drama of the non-specific' (Alec Reid). To look for a 'specific' meaning in such drama is like searching for the magnetic pole in the Antarctic. Beckett's art avoids definition because he believed passionately that 'art has nothing to do with clarity, does not dabble in the clear and does not make clear'. The writer is no 'magus' possessing privileged insight or knowledge not revealed to other mortals; all he can do is distil in words, however imperfect, a vision or experience of the misery and desperateness of life. That, for Beckett, was 'poetry' broadly defined, and it was for him the only thing that ultimately had any value.

He had, of course, a 'philosophy of life' like anyone else, but it was an intuition rather than a systematic set of beliefs. Like the German thinker Schopenhauer (1788–1860), whom he greatly admired, he felt that Will is evil, and that desire is the source of our misery: such happiness as there is, therefore, can only be obtained by the 'ablation' or removal of all desire. This, he said in *Proust*, is 'the wisdom of all the sages, from Brahma to Leopardi', the nineteenth-century Italian poet whose lines he quoted frequently.

Beckett felt a deep kinship with writers like Schopenhauer and Leopardi, and shared their repudiation of cheerful optimism, but it did not lead him to quietist renunciation. Like one of the characters in *Murphy* (1938), no doubt, he heard 'Pilate's hands rustling in his mind' (p. 170), but he did not give up on that account. He wrote novels that tell of humanity's derisory but heroic attempts to conquer the 'silence of which the universe is made', and plays that portray its doomed efforts to master time. The two things were closely related in his mind. Of *Waiting for Godot* he said, 'Silence is pouring into this play like water into a sinking ship': the characters are terrified of silence because silence threatens cessation. The multiple fall in Act Two symbolises this.

As a director of his own plays, Beckett maintained an emphasis on the symmetries of speech and on action punctuated by stylised gesture; tempo and manner alike made few concessions to verisimilitude. In his 1979 London production of *Happy Days* with Billie Whitelaw at the Royal Court Theatre, for instance, he safeguarded the carefully structured ambiguities of the text; at the end of the play, is Willie wearily struggling uphill to touch Winnie or the revolver? And, if the weapon, to keep it from Winnie, or to use it on her? Or on himself? The curtain fell on Willie reaching out still.

For the 1975 Berlin Schiller Theater production of the German translation (by Elmar Tophoven) of *Waiting for Godot* (*Warten auf Godot*), the text was amended and corrected by Beckett himself (often extensively, since his German was fluent), with greater stress on fidelity to the French original and on the network of motif words. Beckett had a long and intimate connection with the Schiller: *Endgame, Krapp's Last Tape, Happy Days, Play, That Time* and *Footfalls* were all directed by him there. In the Schiller *Warten auf Godot* production, the major symbolic innovation was the costuming of Vladimir and Estragon. They each wore half of the other's suit; that is to say Estragon wore a blue-grey jacket with black trousers in Act One and the opposite (black jacket and blue-grey trousers) in Act Two, while Vladimir's costume was identical but exactly the inverse, as if to underline that they were inseparable. They even complemented each other in the way they walked: Vladimir shuffled with his toes turned in and Estragon waddled with his feet splayed out. The result, for one critic, was one of the most superbly balanced double acts he had seen: Estragon was a 'frisky troll' and Vladimir a 'knock-kneed, shambling and blank-faced clown'. Beckett wanted to emphasise that if Estragon's physical resources are greater than his companion's, Vladimir's linguistic reserves are more remarkable.

As another critic commented about this production, Beckett's precise orchestration brought out the play's plastic and above all musical qualities to perfection, a characteristic referred to by Beckett himself as 'ballet-like'. In this, verbal repetitions are reflected in similar repetitions of physical movements. For example, when Pozzo in Act One lights his pipe, takes a puff and says 'Ah! Jetzt geht's mir besser' ('Ah! That's better'), he is echoed a few minutes later by Estragon, having gnawed Pozzo's discarded chicken bones, burping loudly (the burp is not indicated in the printed text), and saying, 'Ah! Jetzt geht's mir besser' (pp. 19, 21). This is all the more pointedly comic in that Estragon, unlike Pozzo, has not had the benefit of a full meal.

Beckett's production notebooks, now in the Samuel Beckett Archive at Reading University, and published by Faber and Faber in a large, handsome volume meticulously edited by James Knowlson, show extremely detailed an-notations of stage movements in relation to the German text, with diagrams by Beckett himself, and offer a thorough and minute design of the play. They reveal a strong interest in pattern, shape and the return of motifs (doubts, sleepiness, recollection, the sky, and so on), as well as in lighting and in the chief prop (the tree). Throughout, Estragon and Vladimir's close relationiship is stressed, for instance by their loud stage-whisper in unison, 'Wollen Sie ihn loswerden?' ('You want to get rid of him?') – again, not in the published text (p. 24) – from their shared position stage-left. Another fine example is their superbly choreographed saunter down imaginary boulevards – there are echoes here of Gene Kelly and Fred Astaire dance routines – as they exchange thoughts about Godot's need to consult his agents, his correspondents, his books and his bank account before taking a decision (p. 11); this is deftly paralleled in Act Two after Vladimir says, 'Let us not waste our time in idle discourse!' and, taking Estragon's arm, walks him round the stage (pp. 71–2). I shall be returning to the topic of Beckett's own productions of *Waiting for Godot* in the next chapter.

In view of what has been said, this play – or indeed *Endgame* and *Krapp's Last Tape* – should present few difficulties of interpretation, despite the many scholarly analyses and attempts at critical elucidation that bewilder theatregoers; they experience onstage a clear and intelligible, if admittedly complex, metaphor about the nature of existence. We may know that the tree (like the dance) is a common image for the isolation and majesty of the artist, and in *Waiting for Godot* Beckett's tree, no exception, shares in the aura of the archetype; but at the same time we should bear in mind that the changes in the tree, like the sudden rising of the moon, 'are stage facts, important only in the way in which the protagonists react to them. Of themselves they have no other meaning or significance and Beckett has no other interest in them' (Alec Reid). In brief, this play can no more easily be reduced to a formula than can any other work of art worthy of the name. Some may declare that it means 'where there's life, there's hope'; others may retort that it says rather 'life is hope, and hope is life'. Both assertions have some truth in them – Beckett's characters certainly indulge in a kind of existential Micawberism – but neither does more than touch the surface of this extraordinary work. I look at it in more detail in the next chapter.

# Waiting for Godot

## Introduction

One evening, on a lonely country road near a tree, two middle-aged men, half-tramp half-clown, are waiting for someone by the name of Godot, who has given them to understand that their patience at the rendezvous will be rewarded. The two, Estragon ('Gogo') and Vladimir ('Didi'), are not sure what form Godot's gratitude will take, any more than they know for certain whether they have come to the right place or have indeed turned up on the appointed day. They occupy the time as best they can until distraction arrives in the shape of Pozzo, a local landowner on his way to the fair to sell his servant Lucky. Pozzo halts awhile with Estragon and Vladimir, eats his lunch in their presence, even grants them his bones when his menial spurns them, and then in gratitude for their society has Lucky dance and then think aloud for them. The three become so agitated by Lucky's intellectual performance that they all set upon him and silence him by removing his hat. Not long afterwards Pozzo takes his leave, driving Lucky before him. Estragon and Vladimir have not been alone many moments before a small boy appears with the news that Mr Godot 'won't come this evening but surely tomorrow' (p. 44). The boy runs off, night falls abruptly, and after briefly contemplating suicide by hanging themselves from the tree, the two friends decide to call it a day. But, despite their decision to go, they do not move as the curtain falls.

The curtain rises the following day on a scene identical except for the fact that the tree has sprouted a few leaves. Vladimir is joined on stage by Estragon and much the same things happen except that when Pozzo and Lucky appear (from the side of the stage where they made their exit in Act One), Pozzo reveals that he has gone blind and Lucky dumb. Then all four collapse on top of each other but somehow manage to get up again. Pozzo becomes exasperated at Vladimir's anxious questions about time, bellowing that life itself is only a brief instant. He leaves, driving Lucky before him, from the side of the stage where he had entered in Act One. After another brief interlude the boy comes on a second time and delivers the same message as before. The sun sets, the moon rises abruptly, the two men again contemplate suicide but without much determination, and then, despite their agreement to leave, make no movement as the curtain falls. So ends the play in which, as one critic wittily but inaccurately put it, nothing happens, twice.

Perhaps the most striking thing about Beckett's first work to appear on a public stage is its maturity. This impression springs mainly from the fact that it is a convincingly created dramatic image, that the dialogue is ably constructed and the characterisation effectively conceived. It is to some extent a misleading impression, however, since the text now available was established only after a number of versions had been tried out. The original French manuscript is in private hands, but enough is known about it to show that it is a rather hesitant piece of work: Beckett was not sure what names to give his characters, for instance, and even whether or not to make Godot a real presence in the action by suggesting, for example, that Estragon and Vladimir have a written assignation with him, or that Pozzo himself is Godot failing to recognise those he has come to meet. These matters were settled in the first French edition which preceded Roger Blin's production by a few months, but even this printed text differs in certain respects from the second, post-performance edition. In production, moreover, Blin advised certain cuts for reasons of technical effectiveness, and at that stage in his dramatic career Beckett was only too ready to learn from a professional. When he undertook the English translation, therefore, he dropped most of the passages Blin left out, and then, in the second British edition of 1965, made a large number of minor amendments to the dialogue and directions which considerably enhance the play's theatrical effectiveness. So the text now published by Faber and Faber has gone through a considerable polishing process in manuscript and in print, both on the stage and off it. When we recall that this development took place over a period of some fifteen years (and even then was not complete, because Beckett went on refining his text for use in productions that he himself directed), the transition from the jettisoned *Eleuthéria* to the mature *Waiting for Godot* was not as abrupt as might at first appear. Although the first draft for *Waiting for Godot* was written quickly, in a matter of just over three months, the way had been prepared for it by *Eleuthéria* as well as Beckett's other works: the model for Vladimir's exchanges with Godot's boy messenger lay in the glazier's conversations in the earlier play; detailed studies have revealed close similarities between the novel *Mercier and Camier* (written between late 1946 and early 1947) and *Waiting for Godot*; and as we have seen, Beckett himself said that the play's origins may be sought in *Murphy* (1938).

Of course, as we shall see in more detail later on, *Waiting for Godot* also has its antecedents within the broader context of the post-naturalist tradition in drama. A few of the analogues that have been cited are Strindberg's *A Dream Play* (1902), with its sense of the hopeless repetitiveness of life and of the unreality of existence, Synge's *The Well of the Saints* (1905), Jarry's *Ubu* cycle (1896–1901; Pozzo is distinctly ubuesque), Vitrac's *Victor, or The Children Take Over* (1928), not to mention the great Charlie Chaplin (1889–1977), who developed his astonishing persona after observing the gait of a drunken cabby. And Beckett is close, naturally, to that other great poet of inertia, Anton Chekhov (1860–1904). Their plays share a feeling of inconclusiveness: apart from the sale of the estate, for example, nothing much can be said to happen in *The Cherry Orchard* (1904). The heroine goes back to her unsatisfactory lover in Paris, other characters turn again to their idle dreams, and the proposal of marriage which Varia had been hoping Lopahin would make her does not materialise. Frustrations and a sense of impotence felt by many of the characters provoke tensions between them, and lead to the occasional eruption which subsides as suddenly as similar explosions of anger between Vladimir and Estragon. A forced gaiety in most of Chekhov's characters masks an awareness of abandonment and hoplessness experienced by them; none the less, like Beckett's, they continue to hope unrealistically for a better world just over the hill. Both dramatists excel in laying bare both the nature of life without real hope of improvement or change, and the subterfuges we adopt to conceal from ourselves the worst facts about our condition, in dialogue that modulates with striking rapidity from the sublime to the ridiculous, speech without consequence reflecting action without conclusion. In spite of all, indeed, both Chekhov and Beckett offer us a subdued form of comedy to illustrate the remark of Nell in *Endgame*, already mentioned, that nothing is funnier than unhappiness.

*Waiting for Godot* shows parallels, too, with some of the plays of his fellow-Irishman the great poet W. B. Yeats (1865–1939). In *The Cat and the Moon* of 1926, for example, two beggars, one crippled and the other sightless, have for forty years managed to compensate for their respective infirmities by the blind man carrying the lame man on his back. Like Estragon, the lame beggar has a very poor memory. They come to a holy well to pray for the cure of their disabilities. The hoped-for miracle takes place, but not through the well's agency; and even if the conclusion is thus happier than Beckett's, the two beggars, with their racy common speech and their mutual need one of the other, remind us of Vladimir and Estragon. 'We have great wisdom between us, that's certain,' says the lame beggar, with a complacency worthy of Estragon.

But these and other parallels are largely fortuitous, facts of theatre history to be accorded no more than their due, which is to reveal that *Waiting for Godot* does not stand in splendid isolation. In several ways, indeed, it is a somewhat traditional play. As spectators we are, for example, launched directly into the action, and the relatively few details we need for comprehension of the past career of the characters are filled in for us as we go along. Vladimir's 'So there you are again' (p. 1) assumes a previous history of association between himself and Estragon which the spectator, perfectly normally, takes on trust. The time-scale, too, is clearly theatrical rather than actual. When Vladimir, only a few minutes in real time after his entry in Act Two, says of Lucky's discarded hat, 'I've been here an hour and never saw it' (p. 63), Beckett is using one of the oldest dramaturgical tricks for suggesting that more time has elapsed than is in fact the case.

It is often said that the new forms of drama (including *Waiting for Godot*), which arose in the 1950s and which I discussed in the preceding chapter, flouted all the rules of traditional dramaturgy. To an extent this is true enough; but it is also a fact that other, later, developments, particularly in the field of improvisatory drama and the 'happening', outstripped the earlier avant-garde, revealing how even in its anti-rhetoric it still preserved rhetoric, and how zealously it maintained the hallowed distinction between stage and auditorium. I shall have more to say later about the rhetoric of *Waiting for Godot*; but the sense of being in a theatre, *qua* theatre, is certainly something the play relies upon implicitly. One has only to imagine what would happen if one or two members of the audience took it into their heads to cross the footlights and join in the delicately orchestrated banter between the characters. The effect would be as destructive of theatrical illusion as on the notorious occasion when an outraged spectator felt impelled to warn Shakespeare's Othello against the machinations of Iago. The existential divide between the two worlds of actors and theatregoers is even, in *Waiting for Godot*, dwelt upon with coy jocularity. With his gesture of gazing into the wings, 'his hand screening his eyes' (p. 5), Estragon is being absurdly theatrical, as he is also in his unflatteringly ironic comment about 'inspiring prospects' when looking the audience pointedly in the eyes a little later (p. 6). Vladimir situates one of the local landmarks, a bog, in the auditorium, and comically sympathises with Estragon's hesitation in Act Two to take cover by running in that direction, despite the fact that 'there's not a soul in sight' (p. 66). Pozzo in particular shows an old pro's awareness of where he should be: 'It isn't by any chance the place known as the Board?' ('the boards' being actors' slang for the stage) he asks in Act Two (p. 79). The play's perfect sense of theatre can thus be explained partly in terms of its self-conscious awareness of theatre.

But it is also attributable in part to Beckett's fine ear for eminently actable dialogue, once the problem of the frequent occurrence of virtually identical cues (which, as we saw, so disconcerted Peter Bull, the first British Pozzo) has been overcome in rehearsal. The vivid, almost conjugal bickering of Vladimir and Estragon is a case in point. Vladimir is the anxious type, and Estragon shows few scruples about needling him where he is most vulnerable. 'What are you insinuating,' Vladimir asks in some alarm, 'that we've come to the wrong place?' (p. 6), as Estragon proceeds to undermine his confidence. His companion's insidious questioning is merciless: 'But what Saturday? And is it Saturday? Is it not rather Sunday? Or Monday? Or Friday?' (p. 7). He soon tires of this, however, and leaves Vladimir with his cruel dilemma unresolved as to whether they have turned up on the right day and at the right place for their appointment with Godot. Estragon is impatient in a general way with Vladimir's restlessness, his habit of waking him from his cat-naps, his slowness in grasping points of logic ('Use your intelligence, can't you?' he barks on p. 10 when Vladimir fails to see why the heavier of the two should be the first to attempt suicide by hanging from a dubious branch). On a more brutal level, Pozzo torments Lucky with a calculatedly sadistic blend of boorishness and feigned commiseration. As for the language Estragon and Vladimir use when addressing Pozzo, this varies from the timorously respectful in the first act to the familiarly condescending in the second. In every case the language shows a pithy accuracy and liveliness, with more than a touch of Dublinese ('Get up till I embrace you', p. 1, is a typical Irishism), but otherwise lacking in distracting provincialisms: a universal form of English speech that is characteristic of Beckett's international background and of the fact that his play was conceived in perfectly fluent French before it was recast in the author's mother tongue.

The dialogue none the less shows certain features which are characteristic of Beckett's manner as we have come to know it through increasing familiarity with the style of his prose written both for armchair reading and for stage performance. One of these verbal tics is the device of cancellation or qualification, which seems to stem from a deep-seated scepticism about the medium of language itself. Molloy, for instance, says of a man he has been observing, 'A little dog followed him, a pomeranian I think, but I don't think so' (*Three Novels*, p. 12), without showing himself in the least perturbed by the *volte-face*. Similarly with Vladimir, who twice qualifies his admission of ignorance about the nature of the tree: 'I don't know,' he asserts, adding at once, 'A willow' (pp. 6, 86). An analogous hesitation perhaps explains why some of the play's many questions (which, analysis has shown, make up twenty-four per cent of all utterances) terminate in a full-stop rather than a question-mark, so that it is hardly surprising that replies account for only twelve per cent of all remarks. But questions diffidently put are one thing;

questions long held in suspense, such as 'We're not tied?' (p. 12), or not answered at all, such as 'Like to finish it?' (p. 14), are another thing altogether. Estragon, for instance, is promised an account of 'the time Lucky refused' by Pozzo, who has said enigmatically and menacingly, 'He refused once' (p. 33), but the hope of further information on this score, as on others, is cheated. Much of the dialogue, in fact, imitates the inconsequential spontaneity of everyday speech, in which different participants tend to pursue a line of thought independently of each other – a technique which Harold Pinter, in particular, has raised in his plays to the level of high art. Beckett counterpoints resulting misunderstandings with comic subtlety, as in the exchange which precedes Lucky's speech (p. 32), when Estragon supposes that Pozzo is offering them money whereas what Pozzo has in mind is a free performance by his servant.

Such comic misunderstandings are pure vaudeville: 'I must have thrown them away.' 'When?' 'I don't know.' 'Why?' 'I don't know why I don't know' (pp. 58–9) is another typical example. But even here the language is rooted in common speech, in which time is lost through confusions over the precise meaning of words. 'Are you friends?' blind Pozzo asks in Act Two, provoking Estragon to noisy laughter: 'He wants to know if we are friends!' Vladimir mediates here as on other occasions by pointing out, 'No, he means friends of his' (p. 77). The dialogue owes a great deal in fact to the tried and trusted stichomythia (alternation) of music-hall cross-talk routines, in which a 'straight' man is placed opposite a 'funny' man who delights the audience by becoming embroiled in the complexities of some problem his partner is attempting, with diminishing patience, to elucidate for his benefit. In

*Waiting for Godot,* as we have seen, Estragon tries to explain to Vladimir that since he is the heavier of the two he should logically try hanging himself from the bough first: 'If it hangs you it'll hang anything,' he concludes with some exasperation (p. 10). The comedy of this is heightened when the initial premise itself is brought into question: 'But am I heavier than you?' asks Vladimir, who is usually cast as a thin and nervous man opposite Estragon's stouter and more turgid physique. A further example of feigned impatience is the piece of cross-talk leading up to Estragon's weary concession, 'Take your time' (p. 11).

Another well-worn music-hall gag is mirrored repetition: both Estragon and Vladimir, for example, almost simultaneously shake and feel about inside a favourite object, Vladimir his hat and Estragon his boot (pp. 2–3), and both men exclaim histrionically, 'Hurts! He wants to know if it hurts!' within a minute of each other (p. 2). This last joke follows the pattern of so many rhetorical appeals to the audience of the following kind: 'Thin? I'd say my wife is thin. When she swallowed a pickled onion whole, the neighbours started talking' (this latter a Benny Green favourite).

A speciality of music-hall comics was the monologue, for which Arthur English was famous in his time; in *Waiting for Godot* it is Pozzo who practises the art, in his disquisition on the twilight which ends with comic gloominess, 'That's how it is on this bitch of an earth' (p. 31), as well as – of course more sombrely – in his tirade in Act Two about life lasting but an instant, as 'they give birth astride of a grave' (p. 82). But Vladimir too has his bravura passages, for instance the comic banter which starts, 'Let us not waste our time in idle discourse!' and goes on to do just that (pp. 71–2).

The circus is another source of *Waiting for Godot*'s unique brand of humour. Jean Anouilh likened the play to Blaise Pascal's *Thoughts* (a seventeenth-century work of philosophy) performed as a comedy sketch by clowns. Certainly the totters, the pratfalls, the tumbles, Estragon's trouser-dropping, Vladimir's duck-waddle, Lucky's palsy and Pozzo's cracking of his ringmaster's whip are all lifted straight from the repertoire of the big top. The amount of gesture in a play reputedly actionless is in fact extra-ordinary. Estragon and Vladimir, for instance, entertain themselves and their audience at one moment by swap-ping hats in a complex routine which leaves Vladimir – significantly – in possession of Lucky's, the source of the menial's eloquence. The hats themselves are a direct tribute to the masters of silent film comedy, Charlie Chaplin and Buster Keaton, and their successors in sound movies, Stan Laurel and Oliver Hardy, for each of whom their characteristic headgear was a kind of trade-mark. All of this (music-hall patter, circus clowning and cinema costume) is taken, even down to the round-song and the lullaby which Vladimir offers us, from the most popular and unpretentious forms of entertainment, where what is lacking in subtlety and finesse is made up for in well-drilled smoothness and in perfection of timing. Like such cruder art-forms, this play must be well paced if it is to succeed: the bursts of action or of verbal ping-pong must really move, and the indicated silences which punctuate them must be genuinely palpable. Where this is done, the play's characteristic rhythm comes forcibly across, and reveals not only the wit, but also the sheer entertainment that resides in a work unjustly thought of as gloomy and boring. How can such a play be dull if Estragon's priceless howler (in asking a question answered pages before, p. 34) is delivered as it should be, with a practised comedian's sense of timing? Or if Pozzo's pompous words and blustering actions are exploited as they should be, by an actor with the large personality and the physical bulk which the role cries out for? Far from weakening or trivialising the work, a director who brings its comic elements out accurately reinforces the play's serious meditation on the vanity of human wishes.

Beckett's self-directed Berlin production – later seen in London and New York – brought out superbly the play's tautness. It may not be constructed along traditional lines, with exposition, development, peripeteia and dénouement, but it *has* a firm structure, albeit of a different kind, a structure based on repetition, the return of leitmotifs, and on the exact balancing of variable elements, and it is this structure which must be brought out in production. The sort of repetition the audience must be conditioned to respond to can be seen in the example mentioned earlier: Pozzo, having eaten his meal and lit his pipe, says with evident satisfaction, 'Ah! That's better' (p. 19); two pages later Estragon makes precisely the same comment, having just gnawed the remaining flesh off Pozzo's discarded chicken bones. But the circumstances, though similar, are not identical: Pozzo has fed to satiety, Estragon has made a meagre repast of his leavings. The repetition of the words in different mouths is therefore an ironical device for pointing a contrast, like that between Pozzo's selfish bellow 'Coat!' to Lucky in Act One (p. 17), and Vladimir's selfless spreading of *his* coat round Estragon's shoulders in Act Two (p. 62).

The entire movement of the play, therefore, depends on balance. 'It is the shape that matters,' Beckett once remarked apropos of the saying which he attributed to

St Augustine and which underlies so much of the play's symbolism: 'Do not despair – one of the thieves was saved; do not presume – one of the thieves was damned.' It is certainly the shape that matters here: the director must bring out the 'stylised movement' which Beckett himself stressed in discussions with actors and others, a movement which relies heavily on asymmetry, or repetition-with-a-difference. In both acts, for instance, Pozzo's arrival is curiously foreshadowed by one of the men imagining he hears sounds of people approaching; and whereas in the first act the two friends prop Lucky up, in the second they serve as 'caryatids' (p. 78) to Pozzo. But the most poignant example is the ending of the two sections, where the wording is identical, the punctuation varied only slightly to slow down delivery the second time, but the roles are reversed: in Act One it is Estragon who asks the question whether they should go, whereas Act Two gives it to Vladimir. The first time round, the two concluding sentences can be delivered at more or less normal speed, but on the second occasion they should be drawn out, with three- to six-second pauses between their constituent phrases. When this is done, the intense emotion generated in the auditorium is redolent of great sadness.

But the asymmetrical reproduction of nearly everything in two acts of unequal length is not the only structural feature in the play. Another is the manner in which the counterpointing of the act-structure is mirrored in the contrasted characterisation. Estragon's name is made up of the same number of letters as Vladimir's; the same applies to Pozzo and Lucky. Hence the partners within each pair find themselves interlocked, having been joined in a complex sado-masochistic relationship for many years. But their natures obviously conflict: Vladimir is the neurotic intellectual type, Estragon the placid intuitive sort; Pozzo is the bullying extrovert, Lucky the timorous introvert. Vladimir instinctively sympathises with Lucky, and for Pozzo Estragon experiences a degree of fellow-feeling. Vladimir and Pozzo, on the other hand, like Lucky and Estragon who kick each other, are at the two poles. Estragon is afraid of being 'tied', Lucky is tied in effect; Vladimir kow-tows to authority, Pozzo asserts it forcibly. The characters, in fact, like the occurrences both major and minor, are held in uneasy equilibrium within this play.

Yet another of its structural features is the way the writing modulates continually from one tone to its opposite. Pozzo's declamation on the night, for instance, shifts almost violently from the false sublime to the prosaically ridiculous, and after rising to 'vibrant' heights lapses to 'gloomy' depths, ultimately succumbing to the all-pervading silence which, as Beckett said, continually threatens to engulf this play. After a long wait, Estragon and Vladimir strike up and swap vaudeville remarks ('So long as one knows' and so forth, p. 31). The transition is masterly, almost musical in subtlety, like the swelling sound of the strings when the brass dies away. Similar modulation occurs between the high jinks of the business surrounding Lucky in Act One and the high grief of Vladimir's cross-examination of the boy in Act Two, culminating in the great cry from the Christian liturgy, 'Christ have mercy on us!' (p. 85). Farce and pathos are intermingled throughout, but perhaps most obviously at the start of Act Two in the clowns' loving embrace which ends, appropriately, in a near pratfall (pp. 49–50).

The whole of Act Two, in fact, shows a slightly different tone from Act One. The cross-talk is of a more

'intellectual' and less overtly music-hall kind; the blustering Pozzo of the first act is changed into the sightless
decrepit of Act Two; and the words of the boy, delivered
'in a rush' in Act One (p. 44) have to be dragged out of him
by Vladimir the second time round (p. 84). The entire
second panel of this diptych is less naturalistic, and
assumes familiarity with the two down-and-outs and their
predicament which permits a briefer restatement of the
theme. Pozzo enters later, and is sooner gone. Lucky's
monologue of Act One, despite its repetitious and garbled
jargon, made a point: that humankind, notwithstanding
the existence of a caring God of sorts and progress of
various kinds, is in full decline; even this statement from a
degraded man of reason cannot recur in Act Two, because,
we learn with dread, he has gone dumb.

Lucky's speech, however, like so much else in the play, is
calculatedly deceptive if we expect it to yield a significant
key to the work as a whole. Those who are perplexed by
the play's 'meaning' may draw at least some comfort from
the author's assurance that it means what it says, neither
more nor less. It is perhaps easier to accept this now that
his other works are better known; easier certainly than it
was fifty years ago, when it was not so evident that Beckett
is no didactic writer concerned to put across a 'message' in
dramatic form. As I have already suggested, even the many
Christian echoes in the play must now be seen to add up
not to any coherent religious statement, but rather to a
meditation upon a world governed by no other divinity
than a sort of malignant fate; a world in which human
beings wait and hope for something to give value to their
lives and console them for the absurdity of their death. For
'there comes the hour', Malone writes, 'when nothing
more can happen and nobody more can come and all is

ended but the waiting that knows itself in vain' (*Three Novels*, p. 242). It is a diffuse awareness of this which informs the bickering, the histrionics and the horseplay of *Waiting for Godot*, a meditative rhapsody on the nullity of human attainment written for performance by an ever-hopeful troupe of circus clowns, bailing out the silence from a sinking ship of a play which is Beckett's magnificently rebellious gesture to an art-form he then proceeds, in *Endgame*, to disrupt and transcend.

## Dramatic Movement and Structure

For Beckett, *Waiting for Godot* represented a 'retreat from the tension of prose fiction', an attempt 'to get away from the wilderness and rulelessness', as he put it, of novel-writing. Being acutely conscious of the requirements of different techniques in different media, Beckett gladly embraced the restrictions imposed by drama; for 'even if you seem to flout certain conventions', he once said, 'there are nevertheless things you cannot do in the theatre, things you cannot ask the actors to perform or the audience to accept'.

In *Waiting for Godot*, Beckett sets four characters, all different and yet all recognisably human, in a dream-country: a bare road with a single tree, a flat terrain reminiscent of paintings by the Surrealist artist Yves Tanguy (1900–55), in which the landscape stretches to infinity. The dialogue ranges from the earthy and realistic to the mysterious and disturbing:

> There's man all over for you, blaming on his boots the faults of his feet. This is getting alarming. One of the thieves was saved. It's a reasonable percentage. (p. 3)

71

The movement in these few words of Vladimir's, from the banal to the bizarre and back to the comforting, is characteristic of the whole play, which modulates continually from one tone to another. Each character, though distinct, now and then drops his individuality and speaks in the 'impersonal' voice which can be heard from *Murphy* (1938) to *The Unnamable* (1953). Pozzo's speech ('They give birth astride of a grave', p. 82), and Vladimir's ('We have time to grow old', p. 83), are examples of this 'impersonal' vein: the sentiment expressed is universal and takes its origin remote from the individual situation (which can, of course, give rise to a personal lament, like Estragon's 'God have pity on me!', p. 69). For Beckett, the only real solidarity for humankind resides in its grief and loneliness: in the cry of distress we are all one, Estragon, Vladimir, Pozzo, so different in appearance, yet so similar in spiritual condition and within the mind. For mind, in Beckett's world, is universal, impersonal and timeless.

When Beckett's vision is expressed in dramatic form, there is both gain and loss. There is the loss of that freedom which, in a novel, makes possible the fantasies, the alogical structures and the games with temporal sequence. There is gain in that the medium enforces greater clarity and concision, produces a wry humour and a rather grim, mocking detachment, and gives the work roundness, slimness and unity.

The play is in two acts of unequal length, both of which are set in the same place and begin at the same time (early evening), and night falls at the close of each. In both acts Pozzo and Lucky appear, but their passage occurs later, comparatively speaking, in Act Two, and then is sooner over. Both acts, towards the end, see the entrance of a boy, a messenger from Godot; and in both, his message is the same, that Godot will not come that evening but 'surely tomorrow'. However, as we have seen, in Act One he delivers this message 'in a rush'; in Act Two Vladimir drags it out of him. This is but one instance among many of the play's asymmetry: Act Two is a development, and not a simple repeat, of Act One.

Soon after the curtain rises on Act One, the different characters of the two friends manifest themselves. Vladimir is intellectual, loquacious and has a more 'feminine' personality; although he is on the whole good-humoured and tolerant, he is excitable. Estragon is intuitive and creative, rather taciturn, and has the more 'masculine' personality. He is brusque and quick-tempered, and the more complaining of the two. We have the impression that he tends to stoutness, whereas Vladimir seems thin; Beckett gives no directions on this point, but they are usually cast in this way and Vladimir's fidgets, beside Estragon's sleepiness, seem to justify this interpretation. Their mannerisms are characteristic: Estragon plays with his boots and Vladimir with his hat. They claim to be free agents, but they manifestly dare not stray from the rendezvous, and every sound makes them think Godot has come.

Pozzo treats Lucky brutally, and is obeyed at once, if not always correctly. The two friends and Pozzo need each other: Vladimir and Estragon need someone to break the monotony of their waiting, and Pozzo needs an audience. Pozzo, furthermore, needs Lucky's menial services, and Lucky needs a master to guide him. The pairs split, however, into other pairs: Vladimir and Lucky represent the intellect (the emphasis is on their hats and on Lucky's hair), and Pozzo and Estragon the lower nature (Estragon's preoccupation with his boots and

Pozzo's baldness symbolise this). Instinctively, as we saw, Vladimir feels drawn to Lucky, and Estragon feels a kinship with Pozzo. Then the pairs divide and regroup, as their names dictate they must:

```
VLADIMIR ——————— LUCKY
| | | | | | | |              | | | | |
ESTRAGON ——————— POZZO
```

The eight-letter names are destined to remain together, and the five-letter names likewise, but because of their contrasted natures they can do so only in uneasy harmony. Thus Estragon and Vladimir bicker and squabble like an old married couple; they have been together for so long ('fifty years perhaps', p. 47) that they are thoroughly acquainted with one another's weak spots. Pozzo bullies Lucky, but is also made to weep by him: theirs is a more subtle sado-masochistic relationship than the semi-conjugal ties between the other two, but in both cases the links are by no means entirely amicable.

The dynamic between these four individuals helps to give the play its underlying unity and its unique quality of uneasy equilibrium: everything balances out, but only just. At the diametrical poles are Vladimir and Pozzo, as the diagram above shows, and the same applies to Estragon and Lucky, who even do each other physical injury (pp. 25, 80). Estragon's fear of being tied (p. 13, and 'no laces!', p. 61) is reflected by Lucky's being tied in real fact. This kind of balance, as we saw, is completely characteristic of the play: Beckett is an artist for whom the shape is all-important, and the 'shape' of the relationships between the four main characters in *Waiting for Godot* is of more interest to him than the characters

74

themselves. That is why the question in his fifth *Text for Nothing*, 'Why did Pozzo leave home, he had a castle and retainers?', is an 'insidious question' (*No's Knife*, p. 92), a red herring which, by ascribing a past and a present situation to Pozzo, diverts attention from the real issue: his role in the play. And that role is primarily to counterbalance Estragon and link with Lucky.

The characters interlock, in fact, with the precision almost of classical tragedy, but in other ways Beckett's method is quite unlike that of ancient drama. The latter, as we saw, is based on an initial exposition of the situation, developments and peripeteia, conflict and catastrophe, all in a rigorous and meticulous order. Beckett, on the other hand, gives only minimal information at the beginning (we learn merely that the two men have been together for a long time, have an appointment with Godot and tend to get separated at night); what action there is, such as the arrival of Pozzo and Lucky, comes to nothing; and there is no conflict and no conclusion (everything continues as in the past). Classical tragedy raises hopes only to dash them all the more effectively; *Waiting for Godot* on the other hand never really implies that Godot will come, so that although the end of the second act is much sadder than the first, it lacks tragic finality. Beckett considered that the term 'tragicomedy' (p. iii) fitted this sort of drama, but its analogues lie further back than the tragicomedies of the Renaissance and Baroque periods in literature. *Waiting for Godot*, indeed, has more in common with the medieval mystery play or the Japanese Nô than it has with the mainstream of modern European drama. Its structure is not dynamic, it is static; it does not rise and fall in a ballistic curve, but meanders and coils on itself. Its fundamental mode is not revelation, as in classic Western drama, but repetition, or rather repetition-with-a-difference: asymmetry rather than perfect symmetry. Because of this it disconcerted its early audiences, who kept hoping that something was going to happen; but they failed to perceive that the play relies for its structural cohesion not on a forward movement but on the return of leitmotifs which weave in and out through the work. The most obvious of these is 'We're waiting for Godot,' which recurs in different guises a dozen times, but there are others, such as 'Nothing to be done' (pp. 1, 14, 60, 66).

Apart from such leitmotifs, Beckett also relies on an elaborate system of counterpoint between the two acts, with nearly every utterance and action having its echo or parallel somewhere in Act Two, as the attentive reader will notice readily enough. In the theatre, of course, the spectator cannot be expected to pick up all these repeats, just as not every note played by the various instruments in the orchestra are heard in the performance of a symphony, but there is so much repetition in *Waiting for Godot* that, provided they are not expecting a quite different kind of play, the audience senses the unity of this one before long. Nevertheless, the very fact of repetition accounts largely for the more sombre tone of Act Two: we have been through all this before, if a little differently, and can expect the situation to reproduce itself to infinity with only slight modifications: this in itself tells us all we need to know about how realistic are the friends' prospects for actually meeting up with Mr Godot. As Beckett himself said, one act would not have been sufficient to make the point, and three acts would have laboured it.

Pace, too, is all-important. Once again, the musical analogy holds good: just as a conductor can spoil one's enjoyment of a piece of music by taking it too fast or too slowly, the director can ruin *Waiting for Godot* by taking the fast sections (such as the hat-swapping on pp. 63–4) too slowly, and the slow passages (such as the end of Act Two), too fast. Tight control must be exercised over the timing of every utterance and every movement in this play, and the actors must practise like circus acrobats until each gesture is perfectly smooth and precise. No one, indeed, should be under any illusion that this is an easy work to perform properly: Beckett demands top fitness of the men who play his decrepits, and also thorough rehearsal to avoid, as we saw, any possibility of picking up the wrong cues and leaving out 'whole chunks of the play'.

The reference to acrobatics was intentional, since it cannot be stressed enough how much *Waiting for Godot* owes to the circus. Pozzo is a kind of ringmaster who cracks his whip and commands the show while he is 'on' (production photographs often show him dressed in the costume of a master of the big top), and Estragon's failure to realise that his trousers are down at the end of Act Two (p. 87) is pure clowning. And as has been said, the bowler hats are straight out of the slapstick films of Charlie Chaplin and Laurel and Hardy, a cinematic genre that also has deep roots in the circus. That Laurel and Hardy in particular lie behind Vladimir and Estragon is certain: like Estragon and Vladimir, their personalities were cleverly contrasted. 'Ollie' Hardy (1892–1957) was the fat, pretentious, blustering partner whose characteristic gesture when embarrassed or in trouble was to tug at his tie, while Stan Laurel (1890–1965), the thin, bullied and confused one, was given to looking blank and scratching his head. Their best work was done in the late 1920s and early 1930s, when they had maximum impact on the young Beckett, an avid cinema-goer.

The music hall was a Victorian and Edwardian phenomenon which only declined in popularity with the advent of talking movies, and it too influenced Beckett deeply. It suggested the pattern, so characteristic of *Waiting for Godot*, of individual turns interspersed with double-acts: Pozzo, in his 'solo' moments, is like the sentimental singer who so delighted our great-grand-parents, or the conjurer who would come on and perform in front of the curtain while scenery was shifted behind it. Lucky's speech, too, is set in the play like the star 'number' of a Victorian evening, and Estragon and Vladimir indulge in banter like music-hall comedians swapping gags. While they were alive, Morecambe and Wise kept the tradition going by adapting it skilfully for television, but it is no longer the great form of popular entertainment it once was: today's audiences find it too contrived and unsophisticated, for a typical exchange would go something like this:

A: I ran into a lady you know on my way to the theatre this evening.

B: Lady? What lady?

A: You know, the one with the blonde hair and glasses.

B: Lady? That was no lady. That was my wife!

Or:

A: My wife's away on holiday.

B: Oh? Where's she gone then?

A: The Caribbean.

B: Jamaica?

A: No, it was her idea.

(A variant on the second example is: 'To Indonesia'. 'Djakarta?' 'No, she went by plane.') Not all music-hall jokes were as feeble as these, but the changes were none the less rung on a limited repertoire of material: mothers-in-law, obese beach-beauties, mean seaside landladies and so on. A slightly more subtle form of humour lay in having A play a 'straight' man trying, for instance, to explain to B, the 'funny' man, the complexities of VAT or the workings of a one-way traffic system, and pretend to be exasperated at B's propensity for getting the wrong end of the stick. As has already been shown, this sort of comedy can be heard frequently in the rapid exchanges between the two friends in this play, Beckett being one of the few dramatists to have adapted popular forms of entertainment to 'serious' drama. It cannot be stressed enough that, properly performed, *Waiting for Godot* is a very funny play. As its first director, Roger Blin, once said, 'Beckett is unique in his ability to blend derision, humour and comedy with tragedy: his words are simultaneously tragic and comic.' There is no conflict between the circus fun of the dropping of Estragon's trousers and the intense sadness of the end of the play. To be able to see the funny side of our predicament is the only way we have of coming to terms with it. Beckett's great achievement is to have cast this simple intuition in the form of a witty and moving dramatic symbol: that of two men who wait on a country road for someone who fails to keep the appointment.

## Forerunners and Parallels

Extraordinary as *Waiting for Godot* undoubtedly is, it is not without its antecedents and companions in literature.

The French novelist Honoré de Balzac (1799–1850), for instance, wrote a play called *Le Faiseur*, the hero of which is Monsieur Mercadet, a Stock Exchange speculator who is threatened with bankruptcy and ruin. He is waiting for a Monsieur Godeau, a former partner who fled abroad with the company's money and who will, he firmly believes, despite all evidence to the contrary, return to save him from disaster. And in fact, when Mercadet is in the depths of despair and about to commit suicide to escape from his angry creditors, Godeau returns with an immense fortune made in the Indies which he offers to share with Mercadet, whose daughter will marry his son. All therefore ends happily, especially for the young couple, who have been in love from the beginning. Curiously enough, Godeau never appears on stage: Mercadet rushes off to meet him.

In spite of this coincidence, and the fact that Balzac could have called his play *Waiting for Godeau*, Beckett had no knowledge of Balzac's play before he wrote his own and so was not influenced by it. The differences between the two works are, in any case, more fundamental than the similarities. Balzac's is romantic and improbable, and is characteristic of its time and of the social class for which it was written in its preoccupation with bankruptcy and the opprobrium attaching to the defaulter in financial matters. It is thus a materialistic play, for no comment is made on the ethics of speculation, let alone on the morality of colonial exploitation as a way of getting rich. Although Estragon and Vladimir hope that Godot will ease their destitution by providing them with food and somewhere warm to sleep, it goes without saying that Beckett's play is hardly about vagrancy and little else. Nevertheless, in their different ways – ways characteristic of the different epochs in which they were written – both plays make a comment on human optimism, on our propensity to look for a saviour to get us out of our difficulties. But whereas Balzac remains within the myth and is its uncritical instrument, Beckett stands outside it and shows it up for what it is: an illusion to cloak our own weakness.

A play by the Belgian Nobel Prize-winner Maurice Maeterlinck (1862–1949), *Les Aveugles* ('The Blind', 1890), also presents distant analogies with *Waiting for Godot*. A group of blind people have been led into a dark forest near the sea by their priest, whose death leaves them helpless and abandoned. A malevolent destiny broods over the play, creating a claustrophobic effect. The dialogue, as one might expect in the circumstances, is aimless and tinged with hysteria. But the play is totally without humour (except unintentionally) and, in manner, is literary in the bad sense of the term.

Beckett is, as we have seen, closer to Chekhov, the poet of inertia, in whose drama, like his, nothing much happens; nevertheless the characters' frustration at their inability to effect anything gives rise to tensions which occasionally break out, only to be disconsolately dropped again as in the exchanges between Estragon and Vladimir. Like Beckett's, Chekhov's drama exudes boredom and resignation; in its forced gaiety it cloaks feelings of abandonment and despair, but hope is sustained in a better world round the corner, even in the midst of a torrid summer which gives the lie to all such hope. Beckett was not directly influenced by Chekhov, but he has much in common with him, for no one has shown better than the great Russian dramatist what it is to live without real hope, and what solutions people adopt to conceal from themselves the worst truths about their situation. Unable to help themselves, they cry out, like Vladimir pleading 'Christ have mercy on us!' (p. 85), 'If only God would help us!' (*The Cherry Orchard*, Act One). Even the two playwrights' dramatic method has something in common. Chekhov's dialogue, for instance, modulates with surprising rapidity from the banal to the metaphysical and back again; as in Beckett, the inconsequential nature of the dialogue reflects the inconclusive nature of the action. Perhaps the most profound similarity, however, lies in the fact that both men are in a real sense comic writers; certainly Chekhov saw himself as such, as did Beckett.

And after 1950, with the emergence of the so-called Theatre of the Absurd, Beckett found himself part of an ever-expanding movement. Jean Genet brought the theatre back to its roots in ritual and magical enactment; Eugène Ionesco transformed dramatic dialogue by exploiting the irrational forces that lie behind conventional discourse; and Harold Pinter expressed in demotic commonplaces myths of exploitation and subjection. In this new theatrical universe, the fact that 'nothing happens, twice' in *Waiting for Godot* soon disconcerted nobody.

The dramatic theory of the eccentric genius Antonin Artaud had a profound influence on contemporary playwrights and directors, notably Roger Blin, but his writings alone would not explain the reaction against mainstream forms of drama from about 1950 onwards. In any case, drama cannot be seen in isolation; the novel too threw up radically new forms during the same period, and new methods in cultural criticism developed to take account of these and other changes in the aesthetic climate. It is perhaps still too early to establish the features of the movement which has come to be known as post-modernism, but when the intellectual history the second half of the twentieth century comes to be written, there is no doubt whatever that *Waiting for Godot* will be seen as being both fully characteristic of the period and one of its most remarkable achievements.

## Textual Notes

### Act One

iii    *A tragicomedy in two acts* – 'a play, combining the qualities of a tragedy and a comedy, or containing both tragic and comic elements; a play mainly of tragic character, but with a happy ending.' (SOED). The play is called a 'tragicomedy' in the English translation only.

In directing the work for the Schiller Theater, Berlin (STB), Beckett divided the acts up for convenience into sections that form natural units, and that in a different sort of play might be scenes. They are:

AI pp. 1–5 ('bloody ignorant apes')

A2 pp. 5–14 ('Like to finish it?')

A3 pp. 14–21 (Vladimir's second vehement 'Let's go!')

A4 pp. 21–31 ('You see my memory is defective' / *Silence*)

A5 pp. 31–41 ('Adieu!' / *Long silence*)

A6 p. 41 to the end of Act One

BI pp. 48–56 ('Ah! que voulez-vous. Exactly' / *Silence*)

B2 pp. 56–69 ('Pity! On me!')

B3 pp. 69–74 ('We are men' / *Silence*)

B4 pp. 74–82 ('They give birth astride of a
grave ... On!')

B5 p. 82 to the end of the play

Note that there are five sections in Act Two as
against six in the longer Act One.

vi *Cast* – listed in order of first appearance; Pozzo is
pronounced Po'dzo. According to Beckett, no
significance attaches to the choice of names: there
is no intention on his part, for instance, to
'internationalise' the play by giving the characters
French, Russian, English and Italian names. In any
case these are not fixed: If Vladimir calls himself
'Vladimir' (for instance on p. 1), he is addressed
by the boy as 'Mister Albert' on p. 42, and
Estragon gives his name as 'Adam' (p. 30),
evidently in order to discourage further enquiry
from Pozzo. The two old companions naturally
use nicknames (the diminutives 'Gogo' and 'Didi')
when speaking to each other. In Beckett's earliest
manuscript Estragon is named throughout the first
act as 'Lévy' (a Jewish name with obvious biblical
overtones), and when questioned by Pozzo gives
his name as 'Magrégor', thus linking him with
Beckett's band of fictional characters whose names
begin with M (Murphy, Molloy, Malone and the
rest). As for the name Godot, Beckett told Roger
Blin that it was suggested to him not, as many
people have thought, by the English word 'God',
but by *godillots* and *godasses*, French slang words
for boots (which of course feature prominently in
the play). One suggestion which has been made
and which is perhaps more plausible is that the
name of Lucky (a character originally envisaged by

Beckett as a railway-station porter), may be a pun on 'lackey', defined in the COED as a footman or manservant in livery; 'to lackey' means 'to dance attendance on', something which Lucky, whose costume usually consists of frayed waistcoat and breeches, does both literally and figuratively.

1 *A tree* – Beckett sees the tree as simple and bare, like the rest of the set. In a production in Paris in 1961 the tree was designed by Beckett's friend the sculptor Alberto Giacometti (1901–66).

2 Hope deferred ... who said that? – the answer is the writer of the Book of Proverbs in the Bible (Proverbs 13: 12). Beckett, an avid reader of Dickens in his youth, may have remembered the quotation being used in *Bleak House* (1852) to describe the misery inflicted on litigants by the delays and complexities of the legal process.

3 Our being born? – in *Proust* (1931) Beckett quoted Calderón, 'Man's greatest sin is to have been born', and the philosopher Schopenhauer, whom as we saw Beckett greatly revered, used the same words.

4 only one speaks of a thief being saved – Luke 23: 43 (the same idea was used by Beckett in *Murphy*, 1938, where Neary says, 'Do not despair ... Remember also one thief was saved', p. 213). On the next page Vladimir refers to Matthew's version, in which both robbers abused Jesus ('The thieves also, which were crucified with him, cast the same in his teeth,' Matthew 27: 44).

7 I must have made a note of it – in the manuscript Beckett wrote 'He', but changed the pronoun to 'I' later. This withdrew the suggestion of a concrete,

real and active Godot in favour of a more shadowy, problematic figure. Similarly, as we have seen, Beckett early on dropped the idea that the men had a written assignation from Godot: a note, however unhelpful, made the existence of Godot more definite than he wished.

8–9 An Englishman ... mandrakes – two examples of Beckett's bawdy, a quality he shares with Shakespeare. The story of the Englishman in the brothel is an old French joke about the alleged preference of the English male for sodomy (known in France as *le vice anglais*). Mandrakes are an ancient fertility symbol and were believed to grow below gibbets for the reason that Vladimir gives here; it is certainly true that strangulation may provoke an erection.

12 At his horse – in the first French edition there is an exchange at this point in which Estragon suggests they leave, and Vladimir answers (my translation): 'Where? Tonight we'll probably sleep at his place, warm and dry, our bellies full, on the straw. That's worth waiting for, isn't it?' Beckett dropped this in the English version because he wanted to keep Godot's supposed promises as nebulous as possible.

23 *sprays his throat* – an old performer's trick. The famous soprano Dame Nellie Melba (1861–1931) used a 'Melba mixture' in a similar way before going onstage.

24 He wants to cod me – obsolete slang for 'fool me'.

– Atlas, son of Jupiter! – Pozzo's knowledge of Greek mythology is not as sound as he thinks. Atlas was the son of Iapetus, a Titan. For his part in the revolt of the Titans Atlas was condemned to support the heavens on his shoulders; he is frequently depicted doing so in European art. On p. 29 Pozzo refers (correctly this time) to Pan, the Greek god of flocks and shepherds best known for the playing of his pipes; Pozzo quotes the composer Robert Schumann (1810–56), who in the course of a long walk with a friend in the country spoke two words only: 'Pan sleeps.'

– waagerrim – at the fifth time of asking, because his question is slurred by repetition, Vladimir succeeds in attracting Pozzo's attention. The way things get dropped, and then either lost sight of completely (e.g., 'Like to finish it?' on p. 14) or picked up again later ('You want to get rid of him?' here) is characteristic of the random inconsequentiality of everyday conversation which Beckett is imitating. before he stops – something of the original French punning on *pleurer* (to weep) and *pleuvoir* (to rain) survives here.

25 It's a good sign – i.e., of a healthy wound that is cleansing itself. By Act Two (p. 58), however, the wound has begun to fester.

– a constant quantity – in *Murphy* Beckett writes: 'the syndrome known as life is too diffuse to admit of palliation. For every symptom that is eased another is made worse' (p. 57). He was thinking in both contexts of the analogy of physical energy.

26 knook – this term was invented by Beckett; it was suggested to him by the word for a Russian whip, *knout*.

27 What have I done with my pipe? – the answer is that he put it in his pocket (p. 23). 'Kapp and

Peterson' (p. 28) is a famous Irish make of briar pipe; a tobacconist's belonging to the same firm stands opposite the entrance to Trinity College in Dublin, and so the name would have been familiar to Beckett. As for 'dudeen', it is an Irish dialect word for 'pipe'.

30 *witticism* – i.e., that Vladimir had longed for the sky to be black ('Will night never come?' p. 29). The French makes this clear by adding, 'Patience, it's coming.'

31 Oh tray bong – French for 'oh very good' pronounced with a strong English accent. It was natural for Beckett, steeped in two cultures, to go in for bilingual jokes; cf. 'Que voulez-vous?' (p. 56), 'What can you do?'

 – memory is defective – i.e., of the classics; Pozzo attributes the relative weakness of his performance to his declining powers of allusion.

32 That's enough! – this has, of course, no connection with Pozzo's 'enough', but means 'shut up', as the French ('*tais-toi*') makes clear; Estragon, however, interprets it to mean that five francs would be sufficient, and is quick to reply to Vladimir that he will settle for five but will not go below that.

 – I'd like well to hear him think – the construction is an Irishism, and of course the remark is typical of the more 'intellectual' Vladimir.

33 *He laughs briefly* – at his own joke, once again.

 – The Hard Stool – a medical term for constipation.

 – What have I done with my spray? – the last we heard of this was on p. 30. Pozzo's tendency to lose things led one producer to suppose that Estragon had stolen them and to direct the actor to grab them when Pozzo's attention was distracted elsewhere. But to suggest that Estragon is a petty thief is to make the play too literal: it is no more about criminality than it is about redemption or any of the other 'meanings' that have been read into it.

34 put down his bags ... Stoutly reasoned! – the question about the bags was of course answered on p. 24. The fallacy in Vladimir's reasoning is obvious, but not to Pozzo. It is correct that Lucky put down his bags in order to dance, but this means he was holding them before that, thereby provoking the query – as Vladimir inconsistently concedes in saying that Pozzo has already explained why Lucky does not put them down. There then follows a long passage in the original French which has not been translated, the burden of which is that Lucky does not refuse (Estragon's question) because he wants to make Pozzo feel sorry for him and so keep him. This was cut at the first production of the play because Roger Blin felt that it was unactable and made for a sort of hiatus in the action. The passage is indeed rather weak, but at least it provides an answer to Estragon's query, albeit one very similar to the answer to his first question (about the bags).

35 He can't think without his hat – this is comic, because we have just seen that the other three cannot think *with* their hats; indeed Lucky's thinking is abruptly terminated on p. 38 by the removal of his hat, almost as if he had had the plug pulled on him. Such is the prestige of Lucky's hat that Vladimir adopts it as his own on p. 64.

The 'think' itself has led to much critical ink being split in earnest attempts to explain it, but Beckett's own characteristically terse summary of the monologue's theme has never been bettered: 'to shrink on an impossible earth under an indifferent heaven'.

36 Puncher and Wattmann – literally, 'ticket-puncher' and 'tram-driver'.

– apathia ... athambia ... aphasia – respectively, 'freedom from, and insensibility to, suffering'; 'imperturbability' and 'muteness, inability to communicate'.

– Miranda – Prospero's gentle daughter in Shakespeare's *The Tempest*, I. ii. 421.

– so blue ... so calm – a quotation from the poem 'Le Ciel' in *Sagesse* by Paul Verlaine (1844–96).

– crowned ... – *couronnées* (literally, 'crowned') is a French academic cliché for the attribution of a prize, and *caca* and *popo* children's words for excrement and chamberpot respectively. 'Testew', 'Fartov' and 'Belcher' are invented names of vulgar origin. 'Cunard' may refer to Nancy Cunard, the heiress to the shipping fortune, who was Beckett's patron in the 1930s, but the word also has an obvious vulgar connotation. 'Public works' (French, *travaux publics*) is a more respectable pun, like Essy-in-Possy (Latin *esse*, to be, and *posse*, to be able).

37 'Conating' is a philosophical term for the act of willing and desiring, and 'camogie' is an Irish form of women's hockey.

– Feckham ... – an invented place name (the other three are real). George Berkeley (1685–1753) was

an Irish philosopher and fellow of Trinity College,
Dublin, for whom Beckett had a high regard.
'Steinweg' and 'Peterman' are invented names that
pun on words for 'stone'; cf. 'abode of stones'
below. 'Labours lost', of course, is Shakespeare.

45 At last! – i.e., night has come. Beckett is not
interested in naturalism, so night falls uncommonly
rapidly. 'Pale for weariness' is a quotation from
'To the Moon' by Percy Bysshe Shelley (1792–
1822); Estragon, the poet (see p. 4), naturally
quotes poetry when appropriate.

48–9 And dug the dog a tomb – this is a German round-
song, translated by Beckett, and an appropriate
choice for a play based on cycles and the return of
leitmotifs. Likewise 'Come here till I embrace you'
(an Irishism, incidentally) demonstrates the play's
asymmetrical nature. In Act One, Estragon was
joined on stage by Vladimir; vice versa here.
Vladimir's invitation to embrace is slightly
different in wording (see p. 1). It is neither possible
nor necessary to note all the repeats here, but it is
their existence which gives the play its unique
structure.

51 the same pus – a sour twist on the saying of the
pre-Socratic philosopher Heraclitus (who lived
around 500 BC) that we can never step twice into
the same stream (that is, all is continually changing
and time is irreversible).

53 Cackon country – another pun on the French
child's word for excrement, caca. It was Estragon,
of course, who brought up the Rhône episode on
p. 47. The man for whom they picked grapes is
called Bonnelly in the French version. He was a

real person. Beckett bought his wine from him when he was hiding from the Germans in the village of Roussillon in the Vaucluse department in the south-eastern corner of France during the last two years of the Second World War. 'Down there everything is red' refers to the colour of the soil at Roussillon.

– like the other – Lucky (see p. 25, 'The best thing would be to kill them'); Estragon's memory is not as defective as he claims.

59 a lot of bloody – – probably 'lies' (cf. 'a pack of lies', p. 43). Throughout this exchange Vladimir has been patiently leading his friend towards what he hopes (vainly, as it turns out) will be an incontrovertible demonstration of the fact that they were in very truth at the same spot on the previous evening.

63–4 *hat* . . . – the 'three hats for two heads' routine was one used by the Marx Brothers in the film *Duck Soup* (1933); it was also a Laurel and Hardy gag.

65 Gonococcus! Spirochaete! – respectively, the micrococcus found in gonorrhoea discharge and the germ associated with syphilis, both being venereal diseases.

68 do the tree – a gymnastic exercise that involves standing on tiptoe with outstretched arms. Soon afterwards Pozzo and Lucky enter from the opposite side to the one used by them in Act One. Although this is not specified in the stage-directions, Beckett wrote to me as follows: 'In all productions of *Godot* I have had anything to do with P. and L. in Act Two come in from the opposite side. They go to and fro.' In conversation

he elaborated on this by saying that they were returning from the fair, and added half-jokingly that Pozzo had not been able to find a buyer for Lucky. The detail is characteristic of the visual exactitude of Beckett's dramaturgy, like Lucky's hideous neck-sore caused by Pozzo's brutal jerking on the rope, and the bags held painfully a few inches above the ground; this is an ungentle milieu, and the audience is made acutely aware of the fact when, for instance, the rope brings Lucky down offstage (p. 41), or we are told that all his bag contains is sand (p. 81).

69 *Enter Pozzo* – Vladimir's doubt as to whether Pozzo really is blind (pp. 82–3) is based on a suggestion in Beckett's manuscript that Pozzo may only be pretending. Moreover, in the play's early stages Beckett toyed with the idea that Pozzo might be Godot, and the assonance of the two names (see top of p. 70) does suggest a link between the two, but with each production the possibility has become more remote, and this interpretation does not now seem acceptable.

72 all mankind is us – they stand in a Laurel and Hardy pose (STB).

73 *aphoristic for once* – the last two words are a significant addition in the definitive text. As for Vladimir's eloquence, he owes it, no doubt, to Lucky's hat, which he adopted on p. 64.

74 *falls* – the multiple fall Beckett saw as 'the visual expression of their common situation, related to the threat in the play of everything falling'. The bodies form an intersection: Pozzo lies at right-angles across Lucky in the direction in which he is

93

to crawl, and Vladimir lies diagonally across Pozzo to form a kind of armchair into which Estragon fits. It must not, Beckett said, 'be an untidy heap, but has to function'. Such multiple tumbles are common in children's games and in circus acts.

75 Pozzo! Pozzo! – they discord, i.e., one uses an ascending tone, the other a descending tone (STB).

77 see into the future – the blind were once supposed to have the gift of prophecy; cf. Tiresias, the seer of Greek mythology. In Berlin, great stress was laid on the word 'blind', which was twice repeated, to emphasise how worrying Vladimir finds this change in Pozzo's circumstances (STB).

78 night is drawing nigh – Vladimir is quoting the words of the same hymn as Krapp sings (*Krapp's Last Tape*, pp. 7, 12).

79 *Memoria praeteritorum bonorum* – intoned, as if in church (STB). The words mean 'memory of past happiness'; note that Estragon understands this Latin tag.

80 he stinks so – Estragon has bad breath, whereas Vladimir's feet smell; this is yet another example of the play's asymmetry.

There is a fairly long passage here in the original French that was omitted by Beckett from the English translation. It contains further discussion between Vladimir and Estragon about the people Estragon thought he saw on pp. 65–6. Beckett later felt that the presence of other people in the neighbourhood should be left as uncertain as possible.

82 Dumb! – note the repetition of this word, to balance with 'blind' on p. 77 (STB), and that

94

whereas in Act One Pozzo was reluctant to leave, this time he is impatient to get away.

85 I think it's white, sir – according to Beckett, the whiteness indicates to Vladimir that Godot is very old: 'If he were less experienced there might be some hope.' Beckett probably said this with his tongue in his cheek, as he was wont to do when making a rare pronouncement about the meaning of his work (see the note to p. 68 above); but it does at least prove that the play is meant to end on a bleak note of utter hopelessness, and that interpretations which suggest that in spite of everything *Waiting for Godot* holds out the prospect of a happy ending are sentimental wishful thinking.

– What am I to tell Mr Godot, sir? – the first English edition had 'say to', as in Act One (p. 45). In accordance with the principle of asymmetry, the definitive text has been modified.

– *exit running* – in Berlin, in both acts he was directed by Beckett to walk slowly backwards away (STB).

86 Ah! He didn't come? – the 'ah' was whispered, in a tone of weary annoyance (STB).

– *trousers ... fall about his ankles* – even at this desperate juncture the clowning goes on. But Vladimir is not amused; he grimly faces the audience as he tells Estragon to pull up his trousers (STB).

# Endgame

## Genesis

Beckett began thinking of another play in 1954, but only started actually to write it in December 1955. Within a few days he had got down the gist of the first act; in April of 1956 he wrote to his friend the American director Alan Schneider, 'I did finish another play, but don't like it. It has turned out a three-legged giraffe, to mention only the architechtonics, and leaves me in doubt whether to take a leg off or add one on.' By June 1956 he had resolved his doubts to the extent of reducing the play to one act, but he told Schneider, 'I'm in a ditch somewhere near the last stretch and would like to crawl up on it.' In October 1956 the play went into rehearsal; to Schneider Beckett commented, 'I am panting to see the realisation and know if I am on some kind of road, and can stumble on, or in a swamp.'

Writing for the stage, for Beckett, was inseparable from performance: the play that was not visualised was no good. He learned a lot from production of his work; as we have seen, the first French edition of *Waiting for Godot*, published before the play was put on in Paris, shows some interesting variants from the second and definitive edition. *Endgame* was published in French – the French title is *Fin de partie* – in January 1957, but the play was not produced until April; by then the author had made certain changes, which he incorporated in the English translation published the following year. Until he died, in fact, Beckett did not consider his text as fully definitive, but felt free to modify it slightly in relation to a given production (this did not mean that he would allow anyone else to tamper with it: quite the reverse). He looked upon his work as a kind of 'playscript' which had before all else to function as he intended on the stage under live performance conditions. That is why he took such a keen interest in the production of his plays; why, too, he was so explicit in his detailed stage-directions; and why, finally, he was so faithful to those directors who, like Alan Schneider and Roger Blin, successfully matched his vision with their realisation of that vision.

Indeed, Beckett dedicated *Endgame* to Roger Blin in recognition of his services to *Waiting for Godot*, since he had been the first to produce *Godot* in Paris. Blin was in fact one of France's greatest directors in the period following the Second World War. It was he who directed *Endgame* in French at the Royal Court Theatre in London (since no French theatre could be found at the time). The first night was 3 April 1957; Blin played Hamm and Jean Martin (the original Lucky of *Waiting for Godot*) took the part of Clov. Georges Adet was Nagg and Christine Tsingos was Nell. Critical reactions were mixed. Predictably, Harold Hobson of the *Sunday Times* liked the play and Kenneth Tynan of the *Observer* did not: predictably because Hobson was always a doughty champion of experimental theatre whereas Tynan preferred politically committed drama, especially the work of Bertolt Brecht (1898–1956). Most critics shared Tynan's coolness towards *Endgame*. The play transferred later in April 1957 to the Studio des Champs-Élysées in Paris, and Beckett's comment was 'the Royal Court is not big, but

*Endgame* gains unquestionably in the greater smallness of the Studio' where 'at last', he said, 'the hooks went in' and the play made the impact it should. No wonder that Beckett was well pleased with Roger Blin's work.

During the next few months he translated the play into English, completing it in August 1957. In January 1958 it received its first production in America at the hands of Alan Schneider, who had seen one of the Paris performances. In October 1958 George Devine directed the London première of the English version of *Endgame* at the Royal Court Theatre, since when the play has had many successful productions and has entered the repertoire as a modern classic; a good director, as one critic has astutely remarked, 'will elevate the work to its proper tragic stature without sacrificing its corrosive, brilliant black comic values'.

If Beckett wrote *Waiting for Godot* in one go, his next play proved much harder to get right. The various stages the work went through can be traced in the manuscript and three successive typescript drafts deposited in the library of Ohio State University in the United States. The first typescript represents to all intents and purposes a fair copy of the manscript, and the second typescript does not differ substantially from the published French text; the great majority of the changes, therefore, occur between the first and second typewritten drafts (both made by Beckett himself). I draw attention to particularly interesting individual variants in the Textual Notes below, but the general picture can be outlined here.

In the first place, the drafts corroborate Beckett's assertion that the play began as a two-acter. As in *Waiting for Godot*, the second act was distinctly shorter than the first; at the head of the latter on T1 Beckett scribbled '75 minutes' and at the head of the second '35 minutes'. In reducing the two acts to one, he did not radically re-structure the play, he simply ran the first act into the second without a break; the original second act began with the words, 'Our revels now are ended' (p. 34). His reason for making the change was that the division into two acts had little structural justification. The second act opened a little later, with Nell's dustbin gone, but otherwise the play continued very much as before. Beckett clearly hoped that there would be a significant difference of tone between the two acts: a manuscript note preceding Tr reads, 'Act I. Joyful. Act II. Deadly dreary'. But it does not come out that way. In Act One, Clov enters crudely disguised as a woman, and a ribald conversation ensues; in Act Two, he appears dressed up as a boy (the boy, supposedly, who had been sighted outside, p. 46). There is very little to choose between the two episodes in terms of tone, and Beckett dropped both from the final draft. In *Waiting for Godot*, however, the two acts did justify themselves: apart from the significant change in the situation of Pozzo and Lucky, there is the strikingly more sombre tone of Act Two. The division of *Happy Days* into two acts can similarly be defended: Winnie, buried up to her waist in the first, is embedded to the neck in the second. In these plays, the second act reinforces a statement hinted at in the first: it therefore serves a clear dramatic purpose. Beckett could be ruthless when he felt that something he had created did not justify its existence according to strict aesthetic criteria; he jet-tisoned whole works because they struck him as 'false starts', and in like manner he abandoned the two-act division of *Endgame*.

The second point which emerges from a study of the

drafts is that Beckett added relatively little to his original conception (the story of the tailor, pp. 14–15, is an exception), but deleted a good deal. T1 runs to sixty-five pages, T2 to only thirty-seven. The early drafts are undoubtedly richer in that they are packed with incident and variety. But they are also more diffuse: the dramatic line is much clearer in the final version, and points are pushed home more forcibly. The characters are more rounded at the outset, but also less consistent: Clov, for example, is a more expansive, a less dry and clipped figure in T1, and Hamm's dread of solitude more obvious and his sadism more crudely expressed. In pruning his work Beckett undoubtedly improved it, but sometimes he compressed things so drastically that the surviving statement is somewhat obscure. Where this is the case, I indicate the original intention in the Textual Notes below.

In the drafts, the characters are simply designated as A, B, P and M. In the dialogue, however, A is addressed as Guillaume, B as James, P as Pépé by A and Walther by M, and M as Mémé. (In French, *pépé* means 'grandpa' and *mémé* 'grandma'.) It appears from the context that P and M are A's parents, and there is a suggestion (which survives in the final version) that B is his son; but the manuscript notes preceding T1 speak only of an 'adoptive father' and 'adopted son'. So Beckett clearly intended from the outset that the precise nature of the relationships between Hamm and Clov on the one hand and between Hamm and Nagg and Nell on the other should remain vague and ambiguous; just as in *Waiting for Godot* he wished to keep shrouded in uncertainty the question as to whether Godot really exists or not.

A final point to make about the drafts is that Beckett had considerable difficulty with the ending of the play; he implied as much when he told Alan Schneider that he was 'in a ditch somewhere near the last stretch'. At the end of T1, B exits, leaving A to throw away the gaff and bury his face in his hands. This is less enigmatic and visually impressive than the present ending. In T2 the last two pages are quite heavily corrected, revealing Beckett's hesitations over Hamm's last great speech, which is much briefer and less tragic in T1. But even the handwritten corrections in T2 do not specify the all-important pauses after 'Old stauncher!' and between 'You' and 'remain' (p. 50). Nevertheless, by dropping the frivolous note struck by Clov's disguise as a small boy in T1, Beckett greatly improved the ending in T2, which required only minor changes to make it into the powerful and dramatic conclusion we are familiar with.

One of the sillier things said about Beckett in earlier days was that he tossed off his books and sent them uncorrected and unrevised to the printer. The falsity of this view is revealed by any reasonably close textual analysis of the published texts, but if any doubt remains it is dispelled by inspection of the unpublished drafts. Beckett was a most conscientious artist, who pruned, polished and refined each work with great care before releasing it for publication. In this of course he was not at all unusual. Gustave Flaubert, the great French novelist (1821–80), was notorious for the care he lavished on his prose. Like any writer worthy of the name, Beckett worked over what he had first set down, discarded whatever struck him as weak, facile or redundant. He was particularly ruthless with anything that did not do what it was required to do: the exchange that was diverting or witty was unhesitatingly crossed out if it was nothing more than diverting or witty and did little to develop the dramatic situation. This may seem incongruous in the case of a dramatist whose chosen realm was that of the pointless and the gratuitous. But the tools are not the same as the product, or the raw materials. However anarchic his vision, the artist must labour to convey it meaningfully. There was nothing inconsistent in Beckett's delicate sculpting of verbal patterns, the burden of which was that clarity of utterance is impossible. 'To find a form that accommodates the mess,' Beckett said in 1961, 'that is the task of the artist now.' It is abundantly clear to any but the most superficial reader that Beckett took his task very seriously. His prime achievement was to have so frequently created precisely the form that, whatever the genre he was working in, would most effectively 'accommodate the mess'.

## Structure

The form chosen for *Endgame* is simple enough: Beckett himself insisted on 'the extreme simplicity of dramatic situation and issue' in the play. In a 'bare interior' bathed in a 'grey light' four people live out their time: Hamm, his parents Nagg and Nell, and his servant Clov. The only event of some note is Nell's apparent death about two-thirds of the way through. Otherwise, as in *Waiting for Godot*, such action as there is constitutes time-filling. All the characters, with the exception of Nell who is beyond caring, are waiting for something: Hamm for his sedative, Nagg for his pap and for a change of sand, and Clov for Hamm to die. It might be a day like any other: at the beginning, Clov gets Hamm up by removing the dust-sheet covering him, but we never see him replace it. He may leave at the end, or his final appearance may be just a routine fancy-dress show staged for his own benefit (since Hamm, being blind, cannot see it): we never know. There are, however, indications that this day is unusual. As it progresses, there is a distinct feeling of 'running down'. Nell dies; even the resilient Nagg falls silent; provisions of various kinds, especially the precious sedative, are exhausted; and Hamm says, 'it's the end, Clov, we've come to the end. I don't need you any more' (p. 47). There is in fact a marked sense of an ending in the play: the word 'end' occurs at least nine times in the text and is, of course, picked up in the title. The playwright and critic John Spurling comments that the function of many elements in the play is

> to lack definition when placed one on top of the other, while remaining, each in itself, as clear as glass. This complex web of references, recurrences, reflections might easily turn into a mere tangle. It is given coherence by the play's dominant and almost absurdly simple theme, which is stated in the opening sentence of Clov's prologue: 'Finished, it's finished, nearly finished, it must be nearly finished.'

The dilapidated décor underlines this sense of an ending. The dustbins, the picture with its face to the wall, the dust-sheets, all indicate a last 'refuge', outside of which is 'death' as nature's demolition gangs prepare to move in. One window looks out on a dead plain, the other on a becalmed sea. To landward, Mother Pegg's light is extinguished; to seaward, the beacon is sunk. The audience can see nothing of this, of course, and has, like Hamm, to rely on Clov's reports on what he espies through the small, high windows; this makes for a strikingly claustrophobic effect essential to the play's impact.

For the New York première, instead of the usual flats, the grimy brickwork on the inside of the walls of the theatre itself was used to good purpose, in particular producing sound of real authenticity and enabling strong lighting effects to be achieved. (It is amusing to note that just before the first performance of this production someone turned off the central heating, which caused the radiators and pipes to click loudly as they cooled off; the critics, however, assumed that this was intentional and praised the originality of the idea, with the result that the effect had to be repeated on subsequent nights.)

Caught thus in their last trap, the characters help time on its irreversible way ('something is taking its course,' pp. 10 and 20) by actions often of a particularly pointless kind ('I did it on purpose,' says Clov on dropping the telescope, p. 18). Hamm has his chair pushed round the cell, Clov busies himself tirelessly with the steps, Nagg pops up and is popped back, a toy dog provides some diversion, God is prayed to with meagre results, there is a short-lived flutter when a small boy is sighted outside and threatens 'complications' and an 'underplot' (p. 46); but none of this is enough. 'An idea, have an idea,' Hamm commands (p. 28), but Clov's feeble imagination is sorely taxed. Material is in such short supply that some of it has to be used twice (cf. 'Why this farce, day after day?', pp. 11 and 20): it is hard to be original when, like these people, you are at the end of your tether.

Hamm, however, has one permanent resource, and that is his 'story'. It provides the play's leitmotif which helps to give it cohesion, just like the refrain 'We're waiting for Godot' in *Waiting for Godot*. There is, of course, no dramatic development of the traditional sort in Beckett's theatre, no peripeteia or unexpected revelations to keep the ball rolling, no elaborate exposition or startling dénouement which might launch the play with zest and round it off in style. Such things, as we have seen, are characteristic of the 'well-made play', and we have been conditioned, in the West, to take them for granted. But they are no more essential to drama than the octave scale is to music. We now fully accept that music of great subtlety, such as Indian ragas, can be composed according to quite different conventions than those of European harmony. Similarly, plays written in a manner quite alien to what we are familiar with can be meaningful to us as drama: the medieval mystery play, for example, or the Japanese Nô. Just because a play lacks development, would we wish to refuse to accept it as valid drama? Surely not. Beckett's method is a very old one, much older than the Western late nineteenth- and early twentieth-century 'well-made' play. The medieval merchant, the Athenian citizen or the Japanese spectator would not find his techniques unfamiliar, even if they might have considerable difficulty in grasping his message. Beckett's drama, in fact, is constructed on lines quite different from, say, that of the French author of neo-classical verse tragedies Jean Racine (1639–99). Beckett relies, as we have seen, on the recurrence of themes, like 'We're waiting for Godot', to give his plays their structural backbone, and where he has two acts he depends on a quite elaborate system of asymmetrical counterpoint; on repetition-with-a-difference, in other words. In a one-act play he has not this resource, so must rely more heavily on leitmotifs and the recurrence of themes. In *Endgame* we have words and phrases which keep cropping up, but the principal leitmotif is Hamm's story. This is first mentioned on p. 29 and peters out temporarily on p. 33, only to crop up again on p. 36. Dropped on p. 37, it recurs on p. 41, and then for a last time in Hamm's closing tirade (p. 49). It thus weaves in and out of the play like a phrase in a sonata. Just because *Endgame* lacks a familiar cohesive principle we should not be misled into thinking that it has no structure at all.

Nevertheless, a structure such as Beckett's is obviously more tenuous than that of a 'well-made play', and would fall apart if it were not reinforced by consistency of characterisation and dialogue. Throughout the play the dialogue reflects the often pointless to-and-fro of everyday conversation. This effect is achieved by two principal devices. The first is the way matters tend to be lost sight of and then picked up again in a desultory fashion later (cf. 'And the rat?', p. 42). The second is the habit of annulment; for example, Nell says 'no' when Nagg offers her a bit of biscuit, only to ask at once what it is he is offering her a bit of; and she refuses to scratch him, only to ask 'Where?' (p. 13). Similarly, Clov says, 'Then we'll die' (p. 6) and then cancels this statement a few lines further on. These two devices – desultory raising and dropping of subjects, and annulling of statements – imitate closely the inconsequential nature of everyday conversation, as anyone who has overheard chat in queues and public places will know.

Apart from its informal, even slangy, aspect, Beckett's dialogue is characterised by the high incidence of question-asking that goes on. Hamm is a particularly assiduous questioner, plaguing Clov like a precocious child its harassed parent. 'All life long', Clov is moved to complain, 'the same questions, the same answers' (p. 6), but for Hamm 'the old questions, the old answers, there's nothing like them!' (p. 24). They fill his life and give him something to say; so that when Clov asks, 'What is there to keep me here?' (p. 35) Hamm can truthfully reply, 'The dialogue'.

There are other features which mark the dialogue as typically Beckettian. One of these is the twisted cliché, that is, a common expression which one of the characters alters, to amuse himself if no one else. Examples are: 'If age but knew!' (p. 8 – the usual expression is 'if *youth* but knew, if age but could'), and 'We lose our hair ... our ideals' (p. 9). There is better humour, however, than this rather feeble sort: Hamm's false modesty about his creative powers, for example (p. 37). Most of the jokes, though, are meant to misfire: Nagg's tailor story, for instance (pp. 14–15), and Clov's wry comment on the audience's stony silence (pp. 18–19).

For this is a rather introverted world: the humour is private, as are the allusions. These, as often in Beckett, are sometimes literary. Shakespeare, for instance, is twisted by Hamm, who is not unaware of his own Richardesque aspect, in 'My kingdom for a nightman!' (p. 15); and Descartes's famous *cogito* is frivolously invoked (pp. 37–38). Beckett's characters are men and women of culture. What else should Hamm quote, as he goes down at the end, but Baudelaire's sublime sonnet 'Recueillement'? For the dialogue is by no means uniformly coarse. It can rise, when necessary, to great beauty, as in Nell's nostalgic musings on the fact 'that we once went out rowing on Lake Como. One April afternoon' (p. 14). Roger Blin maintained that in the French text the feminine '*une* après-midi', rather than the equally possible masculine which could have been used, makes all the difference in this phrase, and he was surely right.

The dialogue, then, is carefully varied to suit the mood, which ranges from the elegiac in Nell's sequence to the explosively violent in some of the bickering between Hamm and Clov. The writing is, contrary to appearances, economical. Words like 'once' and 'yesterday' (cf. pp. 6, 11) have a profound resonance in dialogue which is frequently trivial in expression: the triviality sets off the lyrical utterances all the more forcefully.

The characterisation, too, is carefully studied for consistency. Hamm – articulate, erudite, ironical – is set off against Clov, whose linguistic and mental range is narrower. Nagg, coarse and earthy, is contrasted with Nell, who has feelings, and memories which she cherishes. The atmosphere between these four is electric and can erupt into angry rage at the slightest provocation. They are not made sweeter-tempered by their handicaps: Hamm cannot stand and Clov cannot sit, and Nagg and Nell, being legless, are kept upright by their dustbins. So they all react peevishly to each other. Even their names show this: Hamm is the 'hammer' which drives in these particular nails (French *clou*, German *Nagel* and English 'nail'). There is, naturally, little love lost between them. Hamm and Clov royally detest each other, and yet they need one another: Hamm needs Clov to wait on him, and Clov needs Hamm to open the larder. Sometimes they come close to giving voice to an élan of affection, but their pride and awkward feelings of embarrassment stop them. Usually they address each other harshly and without sentiment, as Nagg and Hamm do too. There is little tenderness in this decaying universe: the characters whine for food or attention, but do little to deserve either.

The characterisation, therefore, like the dialogue and the general construction, is fully consistent with the static, inconsequential, claustrophobic and potentially explosive nature of the play. I must now attempt to answer the

question, 'To make what point has all this art been de-
ployed by the author?' – in other words, what is *Endgame*
all about?

## Meaning

We have just seen that *Endgame*, in common with other
plays by Beckett, represents a radical departure from
familiar theatrical techniques. He has no interest in these:
his décors are simplicity itself, a country road with a tree
sufficing for *Waiting for Godot* and a kind of barren cell
constituting Hamm's kingdom. His plots are slender:
Godot does not come, and Hamm loses his endgame,
perhaps for the hundredth time. Does Clov, at the end,
abandon the man who 'was a father to him' (p. 24)? Does
Hamm, weary of playing the fatuous old game, die after
the curtain falls? Or is the same ritual re-enacted in
exactly the same way every evening? Is it all part of a
ludicrous game in which the man and his servant indulge?
     These questions cannot readily be answered. Beckett's
theatre has its mysteries, its question-marks, for the
author as much as for ourselves. 'The key word in my
plays', he once said, 'is "perhaps".' When Alan Schneider
asked him who or what Godot was, he replied honestly:
'If I knew, I would have said so in the play.' This sort of
answer does not satisfy some people: they believe firmly
that an author understands his or her own work better
than anyone. And of course in a sense Beckett *did*
understand it better than anyone else; directors were glad
to have him around when realising his plays. But the help
he could give them, valuable as it was, was exclusively
technical: he could say how he envisaged this gesture, or
that intonation. He could not tell them what his plays

'meant'. All he could (and did) say was: 'Hamm as stated, and Clov as stated, together as stated, in such a place, and in such a world, that's all I can manage, more than I could.' This is not perversity: there would be no point in writing a long play which could be summed up much more economically in a single sentence. Drama, like all other forms of art, is not paraphrasable. Its meaning lies in what it is, in its shape, structure and rhythms, in the coming and going of the characters and in the cut and thrust of their exchanges. It creates an elaborate metaphor which cannot be rephrased in other terms.

Nevertheless, it is possible, and indeed necessary, to analyse the metaphor. In the case of *Endgame* the metaphor is the stage itself. Hamm, like a 'ham' actor, plays to an imaginary audience. He delivers his 'story' in a theatrical manner, pausing every so often to comment on his own performance; likewise Nagg, in his tailor joke. Clov points his telescope at the audience and remarks ironically on their delirious enjoyment of the fun. We are in a world where all is illusion and all is play-acting performance: we are in the theatre, but a theatre that Shakespeare would have understood: *theatrum mundi*, or all the world a stage.

For the stage, in Beckett, has a particular reality. It is not a facsimile of a middle-class living room, as in 'drawing-room comedy', but a place in its own right. There is no let-up: 'Let's stop playing!' pleads Clov; 'Never!' replies Hamm (p. 46). The stage is an emblem of the notion of imprisonment that pervades the play; there is no way out: 'there's nowhere else' (p. 6). The same is true for Anouilh's character Antigone: no exit allowed until the drama is played out.

If the metaphor is playing itself, the game is chess.

'There is no return game', wrote Beckett in *Murphy* (1938), 'between a man and his stars.' The fates are playing with Hamm a game of chess which he is losing, a game now in its last moves. 'Old endgame lost of old,' says Hamm in his last speech, 'play and lose and have done with losing' (p. 49). Stoically, he concludes: 'Since that's the way we're playing it . . . let's play it that way' (p. 50). He has run the gamut, shot his bolt; there are too few pieces left on the board. Strategy is no longer feasible, tactics pointless: having bungled the game, he's losing the endgame. He tries to resist despair, but he is afraid. 'His assurance', Beckett said at a rehearsal in London, 'is always put on.' His edgy nervousness causes him frequently to burst into a rage. His parents only disturb and irritate him all the more. Clov sadistically reminds him of Mother Pegg and his lack of human charity towards her; but most of all, Hamm plagues himself with unacknowledged remorse. 'A bit of a monster,' was Beckett's comment, 'the remains of a monster'. His 'novel' is thinly veiled autobiography, and he can't let the subject drop. A man came to him, starving, and he tried to fob the man off with reasoning: 'Use your head, can't you, use your head, you're on earth, there's no cure for that!' (p. 32). He was right enough, no doubt, but this comment, uttered by a well-fed, pessimistic intellectual, returns to haunt his last days. He cannot be still: he acted in bad faith and he knows it. Clov, probably the starving man's son, lives with him, a permanent, nagging reminder of the day when he bandied words with human misery.

The figure of Hamm, in fact, is a far more telling indictment of bad faith than the political turncoats of the French playwright Jean-Paul Sartre (1905–80). Set *Endgame* beside *Huis clos* (1945) or *Les Mains sales*

(1948) and the difference at once becomes apparent. Sartre's plays are competent dramatisations of political and philosophical discussions; Beckett's are powerful and vital dramatic images in their own right. Sartre's drama is explicit and rational, making an interesting point and exhausting its meaning in the process. Beckett's is drama of the non-specific: 'don't look for symbols in my plays', he said, because the plays are *in themselves* symbols, with all the ambiguity, the richness and the poetic resonance of symbols. They avoid definition as they defy paraphrase: long after the fall of the final curtain, they live on, creating an impact the shock-waves of which go further than the author could have imagined or even intended. Prison inmates have found *Waiting for Godot* more meaningful to them than to most first-nighters, since it is about their situation: they too are waiting for Godot, who in their case takes the form of parole, or a visit, or just a letter. So it is with *Endgame*. Hamm, who dominates the play, will likewise strike different spectators in different ways. Some may be reminded of the remarkable painting by the French artist Georges Rouault (1871–1958) entitled 'The Old King'; Hamm is indeed like a decrepit king, surrounded by a diminished court. Others may see him as the last survivor of an all-engulfing nuclear disaster, the radiation from which is rotting his bones. Others, again, may simply take him as an ordinary enough man, with the usual arrogance, cruelty, repressed tenderness and frailty cohabiting in uneasy harmony in his heart; a man who longs to bring the whole pointless farce to an end, but fears what lies beyond.

*Endgame* may well appear on first acquaintance to be a black, even cruel, play. But after a while its basic humanity will come across. Of course, Beckett is not a comfortable writer, and he was no happy optimist, but he was a compassionate and an honest man. In *Endgame* he summarised and distilled the painful experiences of the years of war (1939–45) and Cold War (1947–89) in which he conceived and wrote his most significant works. In these he does not humiliate human beings, nor lower them, but exalts them, soberly of course and always with dignity and sincerity. As the Nobel Prize citation put it in 1969, he was worthy of high honour and great respect 'for writing which, in new forms for the novel and drama, acquired its elevation in the destitution of modern man'.

## Textual Notes

3 *Bare interior* – Beckett never had any hesitation as to the setting of his play. On the other hand, the manuscript and typescript drafts do show a general tightening up of the expression here; the concision and economy of the present opening were not achieved at once. At the same time, Clov's 'business', for example with the steps, was stretched out as the play developed.

– *Hamm, Clov, Nagg, Nell* – these names do not occur before T2, and even then are not used in the typescript itself, but only scribbled by hand in the top left-hand corner of the first sheet. For a possible meaning of the names, see above under 'Structure'.

– *Very red face* – this was soon dropped in productions Beckett was associated with. He had learnt from a newspaper report that imprisonment tends to make people red in the face. Hamm and Clov were therefore given red faces (and Nagg and Nell white faces to distinguish them from Hamm and Clov). But he soon lost interest in the idea, finding it too 'manichean' and liable to introduce a note of clownery which he thought should be played down in *Endgame* (just as he thought it should be played up in *Waiting for Godot*). Here and throughout the play, therefore, all references to facial colouring should be ignored.

– *Stiff, staggering walk* – in the handwritten notes preceding T1, Beckett has scribbled, 'James doit boiter' ('James must limp'). In the original production, Jean Martin moved as if his knee joints had seized up, and his torso inclined forwards as if his spine were locked in that position. As the drafts progressed, therefore, Beckett inflicted a severer disability on Clov than a mere limp: cf. 'I am so bowed I only see my feet' (p. 48). Most of his characters are disabled to a greater or lesser extent: firstly because for Beckett, an admirer of the 'dualist' philosophy of René Descartes (1596–1650), the mind-body split is total and simply more obvious in handicapped people; and secondly because physical mutilation is for him a symbol of humankind's serious metaphysical handicap in the game of chance we are all forced to play (and lose) with our fates.

4 *blood-stained handkerchief* – this is also cut; Beckett hints here and in a few other places at internal bleeding, but later wished to see this played down, at least as far as its visible manifestations are concerned.

– *a whistle* – Hamm summoned Clov originally by means of a small drum and drumstick. This was dropped, in T2, in favour of a whistle. In T1, too,

Hamm's dressing-gown, rug and headgear (a nightcap) are all red.

- Finished, it's finished – cf. John 19: 30, 'When Jesus therefore had received the vinegar, he said, It is finished: and he bowed his head, and gave up to ghost.' This is an apt allusion to start a play that is all about ending.

- Grain upon grain – this refers to one of the paradoxes of the pre-Socratic philosopher Zeno, who lived around 460 BC. Referred to later as 'that old Greek' (p. 42), Zeno argued that if you halve a pile of millet, then divide one of the resulting two piles in half and add it to the other, then divide the smaller pile in half again and add one half to the larger pile, and so on, you can never complete the operation (that is, remove entirely the smaller, diminishing heap) because you are operating in space-time: only in infinity would the operation be completed. Beckett sees life as forcing us to attempt, like Sisyphus in the Greek legend, the completion of the 'impossible heap'. In one of his poems we read:

> my peace is there in the receding mist
> when I may cease from treading these long shifting
>    thresholds
>
> (*Poems in English*, p. 49)

That peace, of course, is by definition unattainable, which is why his characters can never die but must go on telling their stories and resisting engulfment by 'the silence of which the universe is made' (*Molloy*, p. 122), until the end of time.

- Old stancher! – note how these two words recur at the very end (p. 50), giving the play a rounded completeness which is characteristic of Beckett's dramatic method. He is fond of beginning and ending works on the same note: see Part II of *Molloy*. His aesthetic model is that of the serpent swallowing its tail, an ancient magical symbol.

– My ... dog? – in T1 this reads, 'My wife?', all hint of whom has of course disappeared from the published text. There is a suggestion in T1 that Clov could be Hamm's son, born when he was a young man, but it is soon dismissed by Hamm as unlikely. In T1, in the same way as Clov wonders whether he will leave Hamm, Hamm asks himself whether he will not drive Clov away.

5 and yet I hesitate to ... to end – T1 is more explicit that Hamm feels the time has come to put an end to things. Beckett's characters (such as Molloy, and Vladimir and Estragon) frequently contemplate suicide, but (perhaps because of the 'shifting thresholds' of the poem quoted above) never seem to manage it. In any case even the pessimist Schopenhauer argued that suicide is a snare and a delusion, and Beckett, who died a natural death at the age of eighty-three, clearly agreed with him.

– you pollute the air! – note the sudden and violent change of tone, typical of the brooding menace of the situation. Actors find the constant rise and fall in pitch difficult to handle: the problem is to prevent the eruptions sounding merely shrill. This, together with the difficulty of remembering one's cues in dialogue as evenly similar as this, makes *Endgame* an exhausting play to perform. But, as so often with Beckett, when the tones are pitched exactly right, all the pauses carefully respected and the actions kept crisp, simple and exact, the impact on the audience is a very powerful and moving one.

Hamm's and Clov's opening remarks show the drift of their relationship and concerns. Both begin with an arresting declaration, try a philosophical statement, personalise it, and quickly come down to domestic chores and similar inanities.

– I don't complain – a conventional reply, again typical of the conversational tone of the whole play. But, as so often, Hamm is not content with this routine answer, and pesters Clov for more details.

6 Yes! [*Pause*] Of what? – an example of annulment (see the section on structure above).

– Of this ... this ... thing – as in everyday conversation, Hamm gropes for the right word and fails to find it.

7 Have you bled? – in this desultory conversation matters are taken up, and dropped as rapidly again, for no very good reason, as in everyday life.
*Clov goes to back wall* – like a child sent into the corner for being naughty.

– I don't know the combination of the larder – without Hamm, therefore, he would starve.

– two bicycle-wheels – perhaps these are to enable Hamm to move his armchair about without Clov's assistance. Bicycles, in any case, are common in Beckett's Cartesian world: they seem to symbolise the body, because like it they are subject to mechanical failure.

– my paupers – this is the first of several indications that Hamm was formerly (like Pozzo in *Waiting for Godot*) a man of substance and property, in a time when such things existed, and sent Clov round his estates visiting his paupers. Note that like Pozzo, too, Hamm smokes a pipe (p. 31).

8 Outside of here it's death – Beckett, as always, refuses to circumscribe the import of his play by offering an explanation (such as earthquake or nuclear disaster) for this state of affairs.

– We're getting on – that is just what they are *not* doing. In *Waiting for Godot*, likewise, Estragon and Vladimir alternate between this kind of optimism and the gloomy realisation that nothing is happening or can happen.

– Me pap! – because Nagg is toothless, Hamm's offer of a hard biscuit a little later is an act of typical sadism.

– Accursed progenitor! – Hamm's language is characteristically formal even when he is hurling insults.

– The old folks at home! – this is a sardonic quotation from a sentimental nineteenth-century popular song, 'The Old Folks at Home', by the American songwriter Stephen Collins Foster (1826–64).

– No decency left! – at this point in T1 Hamm strikes Nagg with his drumstick.

– your stumps – see below, under p. 12, 'lost our shanks'.

– I'm back again, with the biscuit – the frequency with which the characters, and Clov in particular, describe their actions, may disconcert some readers and spectators. Once again, however, this is typical of everyday conversation. It is also characteristically Beckettian in that every drop of word-play is wrung from a given situation.

– Spratt's medium – a type of dog biscuit.

9 Mene, mene? – this does not appear in the

manuscript. T1 has 'the letters of Nineveh'. This recurs in T2, where it is crossed out and replaced by the present words in ink. The reference is to the story in the Old Testament about the ominous warning written on Belshazzar's wall, 'MENE; God hath numbered thy kingdom, and finished it' (Daniel 5: 26). Hamm, who knows his Bible, clearly feels that the words have a disturbing relevance for him in his present situation.

11 Why this farce, day after day? – at this point during a rehearsal Beckett said to Nagg and Nell: 'Murmur. No smile at all, completely impassive'.

12 lost our shanks – in T1 the passage is more explicit – we are told that the accident occurred 'the day after our wedding night. [Our legs were] crushed up to the groin. Lucky it didn't happen the day before.' This bicycle crash deprived Nagg and Nell of their legs and explains the need for them to live propped up in dustbins, but these ribald comments about it have of course disappeared from the published text.

– It was in the Ardennes – the Ardennes is a range of mountains in north-eastern France and an administrative department of which Sedan is a sub-prefecture.

13 There's something dripping in my head – Hamm can feel a throbbing in his head, which he later (p. 14) attributes to a 'little vein'. See above, under p. 4, 'blood-stained handkerchief'.

– Are you crying again? – even the spontaneous and irrational expression of human suffering – tears – is put under the rational yoke of symmetry; as Beckett once said, 'They cry three times in the play, to each his tear.'

14 Lake Como – a lake in northern Italy, chosen for the beautiful sound of the name, which adds to the elegiac quality of Nell's evocation.

15 in three months – at this point Nagg's saloon-bar joke veers off into a full-scale onslaught on the Creator and ceases to be simply a funny, if rather crude, story; cf. the 'Let us pray to God' passage, p. 33. Beckett's own fondness for the joke about the tailor and the Englishman's trousers is shown by the fact that he used it in 1945 also, as an epigraph to an essay in French on the work of his friends the Dutch painters Bram and Geer van Velde. In performances of the French text of the play the joke is made funnier by Nagg imitating the tailor's customer making his complaint in an exaggerated English accent; a trace of this survives in the words 'God damn you to hell, Sir!' (p. 15), which should be uttered in a 'posh' accent by the actor playing Nagg.

– You could see down to the bottom – Nell has not been listening to Nagg's joke, but has gone on musing about the day on Lake Como when she had known happiness.

– My kingdom for a nightman! ... Clear away this muck! – note the particularly harsh cruelty of Hamm's language. In the days before mains drainage, a 'nightman' was a person who emptied people's cesspools by night. The reference is to the famous plea in Shakespeare's *Richard III*, V. iv. 7, 'my kingdom for a horse!'

– Desert! – this is the imperative form of the verb 'to desert'; Nell means 'clear off'. Clov understands this and soon afterwards connects the word with the noun 'desert', since for him to desert Hamm would be to go into the desert outside.

17 the . . . other hell – at a rehearsal in London, Beckett spoke of Hamm's 'anxiety': 'There should be nothing out there, there *must* be nothing out there . . . He wants Clov to see what he's going out into, but if there is something out there alive, it is not as he supposed, and that would be terrible.'

21 To think perhaps it won't all have been for nothing! – Hamm is horrified at the possibility that their existence may not, after all, have been entirely pointless.

– Catch him, for the love of God! – as when the boy is spotted later, Hamm is terrified that there will remain some living organism to survive him. It is, however, inconsistent of him to invoke God, in whom he does not believe.

– Unless he's laying doggo – the ensuing exchange is typical of Beckett's bawdy verbal play, the meaning of which becomes clearer when one knows that in the French text the word for 'bitched' is 'baisés' (literally, 'fucked').

24 Flora! Pomona! Ceres! – the Roman goddesses responsible, respectively, for flowers, fruit and crops.

– Is my dog ready? – in T1, this dog reminds Hamm of 'Zoulou'. This is the name in the novel *Molloy* of a dog which belongs to Moran's neighbours. Such an echo from work to work is characteristic of Beckett.

– a kind of Pomeranian – cf. 'A little dog followed him, a pomeranian I think' (*Molloy*, p. 12). For the Berlin production Beckett changed the breed to 'poodle' in homage to the German philosopher Schopenhauer, who owned one.

- Your dogs are here – an ironic comment on the fact that Clov is a sort of dog too.

25 *The dog falls on its side* – both the dog and Clov have leg ailments. Beckett emphasised their similarity even more by making the Berlin Clov look at Hamm like a poodle, squatting beside the armchair. When asked whether Clov with his physical disability can kneel down at all, Beckett replied, 'He cannot sit either, although he is very mobile otherwise.'

26 Mother Pegg – she is called Cochard in T2, her name being left blank in T1. Between the dog passage and this one there is a long development in T1, running to about seven pages, in which Hamm asks Nagg whether the two old people could crawl if they had to; here, too, we learn that Hamm picked up Clov when the latter was about seven years old. Then Hamm orders Clov to read to him from the Bible (Genesis 8: 21–2, and 11: 14–19). The first fragment, the Flood, is not to Hamm's taste, although it was he who requested it, so Clov jumps a few pages to the next passage, which gives Hamm the idea that he too would like to 'beget'. Clov calls to 'Mélanie', and then returns summarily disguised as a woman, alternately speaking in his own voice and a falsetto. Hamm seems to be convinced that there really is a woman present, and talks to 'her' as if she were his wife, mentioned early on in T1. Hamm, as always, soon tires of his wish to 'beget', and taunts Clov to stand in for him. Clov, too, hesitates, and flees offstage. An explosion is heard, Clov returns to say that nothing has in fact occurred between him and 'Mélanie', and then Hamm asks about Mother (Pegg's) light.

27 That means ... – T1 is more explicit on the point
   that Clov has learnt all he knows from Hamm.
 – I once knew a madman ... – from here to 'I prefer
   the middle' (p. 29) inclusive makes up an insertion
   appended to the end of T2 and intended for
   incorporation at this point. It is thus one of the few
   passages that were added late in the play's
   development. The story of the madman is obviously
   important to Hamm: his vision has come to resemble
   the painter's, and unfortunately for him it is reality
   and not illusion. That is why Hamm corrects the
   tense of 'is' to 'was not' – the insane hallucinations
   of the past have become present painful realities.
 – All he had seen was ashes – in Berlin, Beckett
   directed Clov to turn round slowly towards Hamm
   and show a growing interest in what he tells him
   about the world in ashes. Clov, who describes nature
   as a desert and who enjoys watching the wall in the
   kitchen, seems to identify with the madman; note his
   eager questioning of Hamm for details.
28 A bright idea! – the following exchanges are similar
   to several in *Waiting for Godot*, especially the
   argument about hanging near the beginning. Logic-
   chopping is, in fact, a favourite pastime of Beckett's
   heroes.
29 *They listen to it ringing to the end* – the Berlin
   production showed a symmetry of two heads framing
   the alarm clock, with Clov closing his eyes as if
   asleep.
 – Vaguely – it would not do for Hamm to show
   enthusiasm for something; he cultivates an air of
   refined boredom to cover his growing anxiety.
30 Got him that time! – Hamm is delighted to see, by

Clov's slamming of the door, that he has scored a point in the continual battle of wits raging between them. In T1 this episode occurs in Act Two, and is immediately followed by a section in which Pépé (Nagg) is forced to recount his life story, which is smutty but quite witty. He also agrees with Hamm that he is glad Mémé (Nell) is dead; this incongruous note disappears, of course, from the published version.

- Something dripping in my head – the meditation recurs from p. 13.

- it's story time, where was I? – note the literary register of Hamm's narrative passages, in marked contrast to his normal vernacular.

31 zero by the thermometer – Hamm refers here and subsequently to instruments used in meteorology.

- down among the dead – in Homer's *Iliad*, Hades, the realm of the dead, is situated in the remote west, hence where the sun sets. Hamm is pleased to be able to show off his familiarity with the classics; note the self-congratulatory 'Nicely put, that.'

33 this story – this tirade is one of the high points of the play. In dramatic terms, its function is to reveal how Hamm is trying to stifle his remorse by an elegant narration in which he attempts to show himself (note that he has insisted on having an audience in the person of his father) in a less compromising light. But it is also another instance of Beckett's meditation on the role of the creator of fiction, a question pursued relentlessly in the novels. The last few words are not only Hamm's, but the anguished query of every narrator in Beckett's work: fiction for them is always an alibi of some sort, and a matter of life and death.

The Unnamable, for instance, and the Voice in the radio play *Cascando* (1963), are forced to narrate 'stories' in order to attain the 'true silence'; if they could tell the 'right story' they could cease, and rest. But they are never allowed to do so, any more than Hamm can attain peace of mind. Meanwhile, it is hard not to be impressed by the artistry with which they carry out their self-imposed creative task: Hamm's story has us spellbound. It uses all the tricks of the trade: suspense, characterisation, dialogue and variation of pace and tone.

34 you woke me up – Nagg means just now, of course, and not when Hamm was a baby. T1 makes this clearer.

– to hear you calling me – Hamm does call to him, of course, in the closing minutes of the play (p. 50), but whether Nagg is still alive to hear him then is a moot point.

– Our revels now are ended – this quotation, from Shakespeare's *The Tempest* (IV. i. 148), underlines the hint that Hamm is a kind of toppled Prospero.

35 Ah you mean my chronicle? – Hamm is being pedantic, of course, but he is also trying to keep Clov with him by spinning out their dialogue.

– Keep going! – compare Pozzo, in *Waiting for Godot*, getting Estragon to beg him to regain his seat (p. 29).

36 He's offered a job as gardener – Hamm is still 'getting on with his story', since this is the first mention of the man being offered a job as gardener.

37 Oh tiny – T1 has 'six, seven' crossed out. This was precisely the age at which Hamm took Clov in. Beckett dropped this because it made the identification of Clov as the child too certain.

- I'm afraid it will – it never truly ends, in fact.
- *Hamm raises his toque* – in respect for the dead; cf. pp. 27 and 49. In the latter case, Hamm is raising his hat to himself, since he has thrown away his lifeline, the gaff.

38 Then he's living – a play on Descartes' dictum, 'Cogito, ergo sum', 'I think, therefore I am.' Beckett studied the life and works of Descartes closely in his youth.

- Am I very white? – Hamm, being blind, is naturally not very sure about colours (he thinks the dog is white, for instance: see p. 24).

40 *Head bowed, absently* – Hamm is no longer listening to Clov, but is plunged in his own thoughts. It is evident that the situation is rapidly deteriorating: a good production will bring this out by, for instance, adjusting the tone of voice here in which Hamm says, 'That's right.'

- Me to play – as at the beginning of the play (p. 4), Hamm sees his situation as that of a chess-player called upon to make a move. It is a phrase Beckett, a keen chess-player himself, would have uttered scores of times, not least when he was fleeing the German advance in 1940 and ended up at the seaside in Arcachon, near Bordeaux, where he whiled away the long, tedious wait for normality to return by playing chess with a fellow-refugee, the artist Marcel Duchamp (1887–1968).

41 All those I might have helped – note the nagging sense of guilt. Hamm is returning to his self-justificatory 'story'.

- Lick your neighbour as yourself! – a bitter twist on Jesus's commandment (Matthew 19: 19).

- All that, all that! – cf. 'Be again, be again. All that old misery. Once wasn't enough for you' – Krapp's words, recorded on his 'last tape', in sour reaction to 'that stupid bastard I took myself for thirty years ago' heard on an old tape (*Krapp's Last Tape*, pp. 11–12).
- The end is in the beginning – the source of this is probably that also used by the poet T. S. Eliot (1888–1965) in *Four Quartets* (1944), namely the Greek pre-Socratic philosophers, especially Heraclitus (see the note above to p. 51 of *Waiting for Godot*). It is in any case a very ancient image (cf. Revelation 22: 13 in the Bible) for that which is eternal, continuous, infinite and permanent, as opposed to the fleeting impermanence of individual existence. Beckett was, in all his work, fascinated by circularity, by returns to points of departure, and that is why he found the pithy sayings of Heraclitus so congenial; 'and yet you go on' is Hamm's ironical rider to what is, after all, a mystical idea, a paradox not accessible to pure reason.
- and drag myself forward with my fingers – this is what Molloy in fact does, at the end of his chronicle, which forms the first part of *Molloy*; similarly, 'alone against the silence' is the situation of the Unnamable and so many other Beckettian characters.
- and I'll have called my ... (*he hesitates*) ... my son – this is the nearest Hamm comes to recognising Clov as his son; it is also prophecy of what occurs at the end of the play.
- Breath held and then ... – perhaps a reference to suicide by apnoea, or suspension of breathing, which 'has often been tried, notably by the condemned to

death. In vain. It is a physiological impossibility'
(*Murphy*, p. 185).

42 pain-killer – pain-killing drugs occur quite frequently
in Beckett's work: cf. 'The End' and 'The Calmative'
in *No's Knife*. Hamm, whose only hope of oblivion
and rest lies in his sedative, is panic-stricken at Clov's
news. He must now face his end unaided by chemical
stupefiers.

 – CLOV *starts to move about the room* – this is the first
time Clov has not moved from a to b, the first time he
has shown any independence – humming without
having been instructed to do so. He also asks Hamm
several questions, and even comments on himself. His
changed attitude becomes even more marked on p. 45
when he hits Hamm with the dog.

44 old Mother Pegg – in the subsequent exchange,
Ti makes Hamm more adamant in his excuses
for the lack of charity he displayed towards
Mother Pegg.

45 *loses balance* – this kind of clowning is characteristic
of much in *Waiting for Godot*; there is more of it in
Ti, but it has largely disappeared in the final version.

 – There's your dog for you! – in production Beckett
suggested that 'dog' should be spoken softly (soft like
the object), whereas the other words should 'hit' like
sharp blows.

46 Of darkness! – Hamm is harking back to Clov's
accusation about Mother Pegg (p. 44), and still trying
to justify himself in his own eyes.

 – my last soliloquy – note the theatrical metaphor, one
of many in *Endgame*, which is about playing to the
gallery as much as it is about playing a last game of
chess.

47 It's the end, Clov – from here onwards the rundown, which has been gradual thus far, gathers momentum; Hamm's statement is less final at this point in the manuscript, as if Beckett were not sure that the end of the play – and the end of the endgame – was just around the corner.

48 When I fall I'll weep for happiness – Clov's tirade is charged with the sombre poetry so characteristic of *Endgame*. For him, too, the end is in sight: he envisages opening the door and walking out to his death in the surrounding wastes like Captain Oates on Scott's last expedition (1912), but for less heroic reasons. Right from the opening of the play, to his next-but-last words ('This is what we call making an exit'), there can clearly be discerned a continuous strengthening of his will to leave. This decision was less emphatic in the drafts: T2 had Clov watch Hamm, but not *'dressed for the road'* as here.

49 Wipe ... And put on again – at rehearsal, Beckett said: 'Here Hamm is playing a double role: first he gives orders, then he obeys them.'

– A little poetry – the first stanza of Baudelaire's sonnet 'Recueillement', which Hamm half-translates, reads:

> Sois sage, ô ma Douleur, et tiens-toi plus tranquille.
> Tu réclamais le Soir; il descend; le voici:
> Une atmosphère obscure enveloppe la ville,
> Aux uns portant la paix, aux autres le souci.

> (Be good, oh my pain, and do not fidget so.
> You called for evening; it descends; here it is:
> An obscure atmosphere envelops the city
> Bringing peace to some, to others care.)

'Now cry in darkness' is of course Hamm's sardonic mistranslation of the last two beautiful melancholy lines of the quatrain. Beckett's quotations are not there for their own sake, just to show off, but because (like this one) they are fully appropriate to the mood.

– *Narrative tone* – introducing the last recall of Hamm's story. Although he never finishes it, he seems satisfied that he has got as far with it as is necessary to his purpose.

50 No? Good – in the Berlin production Beckett added here another 'No!' and another 'Clov' to enhance the symmetrical rhythm. When asked to whom the second 'No!' was addressed, he replied: 'Hamm utters his "No" against Nothingness.' Likewise, when asked whether Hamm covers his face here in order to die, Beckett replied: 'No, only the better to be able to be silent'; and when asked whether the handkerchief represented the curtain, he retorted testily: 'Yes'.

# Krapp's Last Tape

## Introduction

In *Krapp's Last Tape*, which is perhaps Beckett's most perfect piece of writing for the theatre, a single character is doubled, then trebled, by the use of a timely mechanical invention, the magnetic tape recorder. This makes possible a dialogue, through pre-recorded tape, between an old man and his middle-aged self, and their shared sarcastic jokes about the young man they both once were. And the technical innovation supplied the frame which keeps real experience at the necessary emotional distance, so that few experiences are more poignant in the modern theatre than the sight of that dirty old man, befuddled by drink, listening forlornly to his earlier self asking rhetorically on the tape, 'What remains of all that misery? A girl in a shabby green coat, on a railway-station plat- form?' (p. 7), and offering with bravado which cannot conceal deeply felt regret the opinion that he was 'well out of that, Jesus yes! Hopeless business', that he was right to break with a lover because 'it was hopeless and no good going on' (pp. 6, 10). Perfect dramatic form, beautifully crafted, and totally convincing in its effortless modernity: that is what strikes us now about *Krapp's Last Tape*.

It was written early in 1958 for the Northern Irish actor Patrick Magee, who had delighted Beckett with his readings on the BBC Third Programme from *Molloy*, *Malone Dies* and *From an Abandoned Work*. There are indeed similarities between the fictional *From an Abandoned Work* and *Krapp's Last Tape*, so it is not unlikely that Beckett abandoned the novel in favour of the play, retaining its best features. If so, then it was Magee's readings which induced Beckett to use this material for a dramatic monologue. The manuscript first draft is dated 20 February 1958 and is entitled 'Magee Monologue'. Donald McWhinnie directed Magee in the première at the Royal Court Theatre in London on 28 October 1958. Good as Magee was in the role written specially for him, the definitive performance was probably that of Martin Held in a production directed by Beckett himself in 1969 at the Schiller Theater in Berlin.

The work was early recognised as a minor dramatic masterpiece. Writing in the December 1958 issue of the magazine *Twentieth Century*, Roy Walker felt that 'the soliloquy has found, for the first and probably the last time, a form which combines the immobile mask and the mobile face, mime and speech, monologue and dialogue, and offers all their various resources to one peformer'.

## Décor

The strong contrast between light and dark – very bright in the playing area, and the rest dark – is central to the play, although in the Berlin production Krapp's drinking hole was lit, as in other productions his way to it has been. The contrast between the fully lit area and the part left in deep shadow is most striking, pinpointing the use of only a very small part of the stage for most of the action, and it is also of dramatic importance. It justifies Krapp's turning round anxiously once or twice as if, Beckett told Martin Held, 'Old Nick' were there: 'Death is standing behind him', he explained, 'and unconsciously he's looking for it because it's the end … he's through with his work, with love and with religion.' But there are also metaphysical reasons for the light/dark dichotomy that may not be obvious on first viewing to most spectators. They have been explained by Beckett's biographer James Knowlson as being a further expression of Beckett's concern with humankind's basic dualism, the Cartesian separation of mind and body (see the notes to pp. 3 and 7 of *Endgame* above). Knowlson quotes one of Beckett's entries in the notebook which he used for his own production of the play in Berlin in 1969:

> [Krapp] turns from [the] fact of anti-mind alien to mind to thought of anti-mind constituent of mind. He is thus ethically correct through intellectual transgression, the duty of reason being not to join but to separate (deliverance of imprisoned light). For this sin he is punished as shown by the aeons.

Professor Knowlson comments:

> The consequence of this view of the incompatibility of sense and spirit and of Krapp's attempts to reconcile them intellectually is seen embodied in the play in frequent images of light and dark, of eyes opening and closing, of light, fire and clear water on the one hand, and of darkness, mist and heat on the other.

He also points out, though, that there is throughout the play 'a consistent attempt made to mingle the light and the dark, expressing Krapp's desire to reconcile and promote a kind of union between sense and spirit', and that 'both setting and costume are dominated by a mixture of the colours black and white'. Knowlson interprets Krapp's movement from the light to the dark and back again as giving Krapp a sense of well-being because 'in this way he came to believe that he could separate clearly the light from the dark, as he separated "the grain from the husks", and still identify his essential self with the light'.

Knowlson has studied the different ways in which Beckett has envisaged the décor in productions directed by himself:

The set has remained extremely simple throughout with a plain table and chair on a bare stage. In Schiller and subsequent productions directed by Beckett, the table was bare at the beginning of the play, until Krapp went backstage (audience left) into a visible, lit cubby-hole or closet to fetch in turn the ledger, the metal tins – which by then had replaced the cardboard boxes of the printed text as containers for the reels of tape – and, finally, the tape recorder. This closet is not mentioned in the English or French printed texts and made its first appearance, in Schiller, in 1969. The cubby-hole was lit from the inside by a white light in Schiller and in later Beckett productions. This rather weak light, invisible at the opening of the play, remained on after Krapp's triple journey into the cubby-hole; it was finally extinguished along with the rest of the lighting at the end. In Schiller, the entrance to the cubby-hole was masked by an opaque, black curtain which was drawn until Krapp opened it. It then remained half open until the end. In San Quentin, Beckett emphasised the sound made by the heavy metal rings and rod when the curtain was drawn. In Orsay, Beckett introduced for the first time the dark shadow of Krapp drinking on a side wall of the cubby-hole.

## Characters

Although only one person is onstage, Beckett manages to have two characters, in effect, by means of the recorded voice of the younger Krapp. In most productions this voice is pre-recorded and then played over the public address system by a technician while the actor mimes the operation of the tape recorder. However, if great care is taken over timing and control of the machine, it is possible actually to have Krapp play his pre-recorded tape before the audience himself, the sound then being amplified more appropriately from the tape recorder. This is more effective since it clearly locates the recorded sound in the machine to which he cocks his ear. The play, then, is only in a technical sense a monologue, in that the same actor plays both roles; but it comes over as a dialogue, conducted between an old man and the middle-aged hopeful he was in former and happier times. Indeed there is even a shadowy presence of a third Krapp, in his late twenties, who is referred to when the thirty-nine-year-old Krapp mentions 'these old P[ost].-M[ortem].s' which he usually indulges in, as indeed does the old Krapp also, 'before embarking on a new . . . retrospect' (p. 6).

Krapp's purple nose is due to his drinking, of course. His shabby garb not only reveals his present poverty and neglect, it also shows him as a clown (the white face and boots especially, and the slipping on the banana skin), and thus links him to other Beckettian clown figures, such as Estragon and Clov; cf. 'played the clown, all alone, hour after hour, motionless . . . spell-bound, groaning' (*Malone Dies*, p. 195). It is interesting to note, however, that in the Berlin production the external clownish indications – the purple nose, trousers too short, boots too big and the four capacious pockets – were cut out. This made it all the more necessary for Martin Held to emphasise the clown in his performance. Krapp's poor sight is something that Beckett himself was familiar with, since he suffered from cataracts for several years and is thus making a wry joke at his own expense.

## Structure

This looks complicated when the play is read in an armchair, but is perfectly straightforward in performance. Old Krapp opens in his own voice; the middle-aged Krapp then speaks on tape; Krapp senior stops him, croaks out a fragment of a hymn, resumes his listening, interrupts it again to consult the dictionary, listens further, switches off when the younger man announces the imminent end of the tape and winds back to the account of the 'farewell to love'. Then Krapp the elder records his own comments, sings his hymn again, remembers the love story, throws away his current recording (the 'last tape' of the title), returns for the third time to the love affair, and this time allows the tape to be concluded and 'run on in silence'. The structure is thus one of counterpoint, with more time given to the younger man's tape and less to Krapp's last tape.

Many critics have congratulated Beckett on his imaginative dramatic use of the tape recorder, and several point out that this enables him to return to something explored in his first book, *Proust* (1931), the problem of the ever-changing identity of the self. Thus Hugh Kenner is moved to describe *Krapp's Last Tape* as a 'last bitter parody of those vases celebrated in *Proust*, where the lost past is sealed away', and Michael Robinson points out that Beckett has brilliantly overcome the problem of incorporating material from the past into the play and has 'fashioned a vehicle which manages to combine, not only the background which drama normally requires, but also the Proustian past of an individual in time'.

## Textual Notes

Although Irish names and references creep in (for instance, the mother's death in a nursing home, pp. 8–9), there does not seem to be anything specifically Irish about the language of *Krapp's Last Tape*. Krapp is not as self-conscious about his use of language as, say, Hamm is, but he does show a writer's enjoyment of words and sensitivity to them. Beckett uses this latter characteristic as a means of distinguishing between the Krapp that we see and the one that we hear on tape. The language of Krapp the younger is more learned and even precious compared with Krapp senior's: note the latter's irritation at the former's pompous, pedantic style, and his stopping the tape whenever the younger Krapp begins to declaim. He fails to understand the word 'viduity' (p. 8) used by his former self; on the other hand, even at sixty-nine Krapp can still revel child-like in the joys of a word like 'spool', with its sensuous plosive and its elongated vowel (p. 4). But, as Alec Reid has pointed out, the language of the play operates on another important level:

As we listen, we become aware of something else, of three distinct sound patterns. Gradually we distinguish an even-paced measure for narrative speech, a slower, long-drawn-out lyrical tempo, and a brisker, harsh, sardonic tone, and we notice the periods of silence marking the change from one rhythm to the next. From the interplay of these rhythms we gradually realise that Krapp-at-69 is torn by two radically opposed elements in his character, and that the conflict still racks the old man sitting at the table in front of us. The sound patterns do not depend on any 'interpretation' imposed by the actor or the director. They are inevitable; deliberately constructed by Beckett through the words he has chosen, the way he has arranged them, and the pauses which he has put down to separate them.

(*All I Can Manage*, pp. 21–2)

3 *A late evening in the future* – Beckett was forestalling the reviewer's quibble that, as the invention of the magnetic tape recorder was a fairly recent development in 1958, it was not possible then for an old man to listen to tapes recorded in his youth, i.e., in the 1920s.

– *a wearish old man* – 'wearish' means feeble, withered, shrunk.

– *remains a moment motionless* – note the extended mime of this opening section. In performance, especially for television, it has usually been modified: in the German production with Martin Held, for instance, there was only one drawer at the side of the table, and the envelope and keys were omitted. Indeed, in all productions in which Beckett was involved much of the stage 'business' was cut out.

5 Mother at rest at last ... The black ball ... – this is both a précis of the tape we are about to listen to with Krapp and a haunting image in itself, as James

Knowlson points out: 'Here images of darkness are not only associated with death, but also juxtaposed with images of whiteness. In giving the black ball to the white dog, apparent opposites are integrated one with the other'; and he goes on to quote Beckett himself as saying that the gesture of giving the ball to the dog 'is one of sacrificing sense to spirit', the form here too being that of mingling.

- Slight improvement in bowel condition – the juxtaposition of this with the preceding and following items in Krapp's list is bound to have a comic effect on stage. Constipation is an appropriate affliction for a man of this name, although it should be noticed that a character in the abandoned play *Eleuthéria* is called Monsieur Victor Krap.

- Memorable equinox? – this may have a sexual significance for Krapp senior; cf. Watt's 'biannual equinoctial nocturnal emission in vacuo' (*Watt*, p. 232). But for Krapp junior it is a religious or aesthetic notion: see below the note to 'the vision at last', p. 9. James Knowlson considers that the phrase is included because it evokes a perfect balance of light and darkness, since the dictionary definition of 'equinox' is the moment at which the sun crosses the celestial equator in March and in September, making the day and the night of equal length.

- Farewell to ... love – it is easy to visualise the comic effect of short-sighted Krapp poring over the large ledger and finally dropping flatly the word 'love'. It is not without significance that 'Farewell to Love' is the title of a poem by John Donne (1572–1631).

- *hand cupping ear towards machine* – in Berlin, Beckett dropped this gesture and instead made Held emphasise Krapp's overall listening posture.
  my old weakness – does he mean his fondness for bananas, or for alcohol? James Knowlson inclines to the view that what is being referred to here is a more or less permanent problem with his bowel movements.
- crest of the wave – or thereabouts – a characteristically comic qualification: note the cliché, followed by hesitation, than bathos.
- the awful occasion – his birth; Krapp is not alone among Beckett's characters in this feeling. Cf. Mr Tyler in *All That Fall* (1957), 'I was cursing the wet Saturday afternoon of my conception' (p. 175), and Neary in *Murphy* (1938), who cursed in turn 'first the day in which he was born, then – in a bold flash-back – the night in which he was conceived' (p. 46).
6 Cut 'em out! – he is still talking about bananas, which cause constipation.
- light ... darkness – see comments under 'Décor' above.
- Connaught – a province in the west of Ireland. In the San Quentin production (1977) Beckett changed this to 'Kerry' because the American actor Rick Cluchey had difficulty pronouncing the name.
  Bianca in Kedar Street – there is no such street in Dublin or London, nor does it seem to be an anagram for Drake Street. Perhaps it is an anagram of 'Darke', in contrast to the girl's name, Bianca, which means 'white' in Italian; cf. the heroine in *More Pricks Than Kicks* (1934) called 'the Alba'

(also, literally, 'the white one' in Italian, to whom
the poem of 1935 entitled 'Alba' is addressed);
indeed, in an early draft of the play Bianca was
called Alba. While there is clearly much play here
on the light-and-darkness motif (in Hebrew, for
instance, 'kedar' means 'black'), there are strong
autobiographical elements too, which help account
for the work's poignancy and pathos. 'The Alba'
has been identified as Ethna MacCarthy and the
'green one' as Peggy Sinclair, two young women
with whom Beckett was in love in his late twenties.

6–7  *Brief laugh* – note how the two Krapps laugh
together over the youthfulness of their self on the
earliest of the tapes. The Berlin production
underlined a deliberate symmetry in Krapp's
intermittent laughs; first he laughed once, then
twice, then four times but alone. This mechanical
sequence stands in sharp contrast to a liberating
laugh: it is a laugh into the void. His laugh is also
self-mocking because nothing essential has changed
during the thirty years since the recording was
made.

7  A girl in a shabby green coat – cf. 'the Smeraldina'
(Italian for 'the little emerald'), another of the
heroines in *More Pricks Than Kicks*, and cf. 'the
green one' in *Eh Joe* (1966). The real person behind
the name was Peggy Sinclair (see under p. 6, above).
Note too that Beckett's mother, like Krapp's, died
after a 'long viduity'; in her case it lasted from 1933,
the year Beckett's father died when Beckett himself
was (like Krapp) in his late twenties, until 1950.
The young Sam gave 'the green girl' Peggy Sinclair
the nickname Smeraldina ('little emerald') because

she was Irish, had greenish eyes and wore green. 'All that misery' refers, of course, to the anguish of first love, which Beckett and Peggy experienced together: as a perceptive French saying (which might almost serve as an epigraph to *Krapp's Last Tape*) puts it, 'you only love once, the first time'.

– Now the day is over – from the hymn by Sabine Baring-Gould (1834–1924), who also wrote 'Onward, Christian Soldiers'. Beckett's devout Protestant upbringing accounts for his precise recollections of this form of popular verse. Note too that this is another instance of 'darkness'. Beckett later felt, however, that the allusion was too self-conscious and omitted it from productions with which he was associated.

– the old eye to come – the eye of the future Krapp, whom we see before us on the stage.

– the canal – the Dublin Grand Canal crops up in several of Beckett's works, such as the short story 'First Love' (1946) and the novel *Malone Dies* (1951). 'The house' was in real life the Merrion Nursing Home, where Beckett's mother died, a top window of which could be seen from the canal bank.

– lay a-dying – while this is an example of the pompous speech of the earlier Krapp that irritates the old Krapp, it also alludes to the lines 'Old Time is still a-flying ... Tomorrow will be dying' in the famous poem by Robert Herrick (1591–1674), *To the Virgins, to Make Much of Time*, which begins 'Gather ye Rose-buds while ye may'. As always, Beckett's literary allusions are apt.

8 vidua-bird – there are a number of species, like the

weaver-bird, in the genus *Vidua*; the male's breeding plumage is a sombre black. As James Knowlson points out, the definition which Krapp looks up does not appear to be from any standard dictionary; it contains additional information which adds considerably to the resonance of the definition. 'Viduity' is extended to include men, women, animals and birds, and 'black plumage of male' offers yet another sombre death image: the Portuguese are said to call this bird 'the widow' from its colour and its long tail-feathers, which resemble the train of a widow's mourning robes.

- the blind went down – a traditional signal that a death has occurred. Cf. the haunting line in 'Anthem for Doomed Youth' by Wilfred Owen (1893–1918): 'And each slow dusk a drawing-down of blinds'.

9 until my dying day – the subdued yet intense emotion of this remark shows that Krapp's longing for his mother to be 'gone' (p. 8) was not callousness; in any case, on p. 11 he says he himself is 'burning to be gone'. Krapp is, in fact, untypical of Beckett's heroes for the tenderness revealed in this passage and in the later description of love in a boat.

- the vision at last – this 'memorable equinox' appears to have been for Krapp the occasion of a religious or aesthetic illumination of some kind, very similar to one which Beckett himself experienced at the same age (the 'jetty' was in real life the East Pier at Dun Laoghaire). It was clearly a key memory: Krapp believed that this vision had revealed a way of reconciling light and dark, and that the revelation would transform his life and work. But the old Krapp cannot bear to listen to this account of the vision, to which he reacts with impatience and anger. The only passage that interests him is 'my face in her breasts', and he winds back eagerly to hear the beginning of the story.

10 after a few moments she did – cf. the emphasis on 'moments' at the time of his mother's death (pp. 8–9). 'Let me in' has an unfortunate, and unintended, sexual connotation; the French translation 'm'ont laissé entrer', 'they [her eyes] let me in', makes the meaning clear, i.e., her eyes opened to let him into her innermost soul. As for 'flags', this is another word for rushes.

11 The eyes she had! – even cynical old Krapp is betrayed into an elegiac utterance here. He has always been moved by women's eyes, though: cf. p. 6 (Bianca's eyes), and p. 8 (the nurse who had eyes like chrysolite; see *Othello*, V. ii. 145).

– old muckball – our planet.

– the sour cud and the iron stool – indigestion and constipation respectively; cf. 'The Hard Stool', *Waiting for Godot*, p. 33.

– Seventeen copies sold – not a brilliant total for the 'opus magnum' (p. 7), the 'great work', which, one assumes, was engendered by the vision on the night of the memorable equinox. The price of the book was the same as the standard basic solicitor's fee before the Second World War; the equivalent in decimal currency of this sum, £1 6s 8d, expressed to the nearest penny, is £1.33.

– reading *Effie* again – *Effi Briest* (1895) is a famous

novel about provincial adultery by the German author Theodor Fontane (1819–98). It tells how the young wife of a Prussian civil servant, stationed on the Baltic coast, takes to meeting her officer lover in the sand dunes, and how she later comes to a tragic end. The book – also mentioned in *All That Fall*, p. 189 – was one of Beckett's favourites. It is, indeed, a very sad story, but it is characteristic of both Krapp and his creator that the delicate evocation of young Effi should be undercut by the coarse reflections upon Fanny's visits soon afterwards. In his own productions Beckett made Krapp's masturbatory inclinations more explicit by changing 'better than a kick in the crutch' (p. 12) to 'better than the thumb and forefinger'.

12 in the dingle – a dingle is a wooded hollow or dell. 'With the bitch' refers to something alluded to also in one of Beckett's early poems in English, 'Serena II' (1935), which commemorates a similar walk in the hills near Dublin with a much-loved Kerry Blue terrier bitch.

– *winds [tape] forward* – this direction (found in some editions) is of course a mistake; it should read 'back'.

– – gooseberries, she said ... – this is repeated verbatim from p. 10, not only to extract extra pathos from it, but also because, as we saw with the two acts of *Waiting for Godot*, Beckett's dramatic technique relies heavily on repetition and *da capo*; cf. *Play* (1963), the performance of which must be 'repeated exactly'. Note that this time Krapp hears it through to the end, only moving his lips as if attempting to say something. As S. E. Gontarski, the critic who has paid closest attention to the work's evolution, points out, the play became, as Beckett shaped it, 'a study of recurrent failure more universal than sexual inadequacy', a portrait of 'a beaten man who now curses his younger selves at least in part for the decision to abandon love', and that 'the final masterful patho-comic balance was achieved [only] through careful revision'.

13 Not with the fire in me now – the thirty-nine-year-old Krapp rejected happiness for the 'fire in him', by which he means the creative energy and insight engendered by his experience at the time of the 'memorable equinox'. The old Krapp shows only too clearly the dismal consequences of his ascetic 'farewell to ... love' (p. 5): the 'fire' to which he accorded a higher priority is now not even a glow in the embers. On the other hand we are well aware that had Krapp opted for ordinary happiness it would in any case by now long since have turned to ashes. The paradox is that the decision confronting him was in fact a non-choice: as a writer he was not in a position to prefer such ordinary happiness, which for Beckettian man is of neither this world nor the next; that is why Krapp, like the tape, runs on finally into silence. This was underscored, in some of Beckett's own productions, by the striking image, in a set otherwise plunged into darkness, of Krapp's face picked out at the end by the reflection of a small beam of light playing off the rotating spool as it runs on in silence. In other Beckett productions, all the lights were slowly faded until the tape recorder's 'magic eye' was all that was visible as the curtain fell.

# Chronology

1906   Samuel Barclay Beckett born at Foxrock, near
Dublin, on 13 April, second son of William Frank
Beckett, a quantity surveyor, and his wife Mary, *née*
Roe. Kindergarten: Miss Ida Elsner's Academy,
Stillorgan; prep school: Earlsfort House School,
Dublin; public school: Portora Royal, Enniskillen.

1923–7   Trinity College, Dublin; top first in French and
Italian; large gold medal.

1928   Spends first two terms teaching at Campbell
College, Belfast.

1928–30   Exchange lector at the École Normale
Supérieure in Paris. Meets James Joyce. Has first
poems published.

1930–32   Assistant lecturer in French, Trinity College,
Dublin. Resigns after four terms.

1932–7   Years of study and travel, mainly in Germany.

1937   Settles permanently in Paris.

1942   Resistance group in which Beckett is active is
betrayed to the Gestapo; Beckett escapes to the
south of France.

1942–5   Lives in hiding in the village of Roussillon
(Vaucluse department).

1945–6 Works as storekeeper and interpreter with the Irish Red Cross hospital in Saint-Lô (Normandy).

1946 Back in Paris, writes the novel trilogy and *Waiting for Godot* in French.

1953 Première in Paris of *Waiting for Godot*.

1955 Première in London of *Waiting for Godot*.

1957 Première in London of *Endgame* in French.

1958 Première in London of *Endgame* in English and of *Krapp's Last Tape*.

1969 Nobel Prize for Literature.

1989 Dies in Paris; buried in Montparnasse cemetery.

# Select Bibliography

Only major studies are listed, chiefly those quoted in the text; for other titles, see the bibliographies in these books

Abel, Lionel. *Metatheatre* (New York: Hill & Wang, 1963) is a ground-breaking study of 'metatheatre', i.e. drama that is self-conscious and reflects upon itself as drama. As I have argued in the introduction to my book, much of what Lionel Abel has to say about metatheatre can be applied to the plays of Samuel Beckett.

Esslin, Martin. *The Theatre of the Absurd* (Harmondsworth: Penguin, 1968) is another ground-breaking study, this time of the so-called 'Theatre of the Absurd', a term which Martin Esslin popularised; the chapter on Beckett places his work in the context of the wider theatrical movement which in the 1950s challenged the traditional 'well-made' play.

Kenner, Hugh. *Samuel Beckett: A Critical Study* (New York: Grove Press, 1961) is one of the earliest and cleverest studies of Beckett's work. This highly readable book was the first to explore Beckett's debt to Descartes and thereby throw light on the thinking underlying the novels and plays.

Knowlson, James. *Damned to Fame: The Life of Samuel Beckett* (London: Bloomsbury, 1996) is the definitive biography, written by an old friend of Beckett's with his blessing and with the benefit of unique access to private papers and to people who knew the playwright. James Knowlson's sympathetic but not adulatory study is unlikely to be surpassed for many decades to come.

Knowlson, James, gen. ed. *The Theatrical Notebooks of Samuel Beckett* (London: Faber & Faber, 1994). The Samuel Beckett archive at Reading University, founded by James Knowlson with generous gifts from the playwright, contains the notebooks kept by Beckett when he was directing his own plays. They have been superbly edited by James Knowlson and others, and they offer both an indispensable aid to the understanding of the works concerned and a unique resource for serious students of all drama. What would one not give for similar notebooks kept by Shakespeare, revealing the Bard's working methods! But alas, such valuable documents are unlikely ever to come to light, so we must be grateful that Beckett's have been preserved.

Reid, Alec. *All I Can Manage, More Than I Could* (Dublin: Dolmen Press, 1968) is a short, very readable study by an Irish critic and man of the theatre which throws valuable light on Beckett's working methods and is a helpful introduction to his dramatic works.

Spurling, John, and John Fletcher. *Beckett: A Study of His Plays* (London: Methuen, 1972). The chapters by John Spurling are of particular interest, since he is a practising dramatist who owes much to, and has been greatly influenced by, the plays of Samuel Beckett.